DEVOTIONS ON THE
Small Catechism

CONCORDIA PUBLISHING HOUSE · SAINT LOUIS

Concordia
Publishing House

Founded in 1869 as the publishing arm of The Lutheran
Church—Missouri Synod, Concordia Publishing House gives
all glory to God for the blessing of 150 years of opportunities
to provide resources that are faithful to the Holy Scriptures
and the Lutheran Confessions.

Copyright © 2019 Concordia Publishing House
3558 S. Jefferson Avenue, St Louis, MO 63118-3968
1-800-325-3040 • cph.org

Manufactured in the United States of America

Library of Congress Cataloging-in-Publication Data

Names: Concordia Publishing House.
Title: Devotions on the Small Catechism.
Description: Saint Louis : Concordia Publishing House, 2019.
Identifiers: LCCN 2018036647 (print) | LCCN 2018053863 (ebook) | ISBN
 9780758661999 | ISBN 9780758661982
Subjects: LCSH: Luther, Martin, 1483-1546. Kleine Katechismus. | Devotional
 literature.
Classification: LCC BX8070.L8 (ebook) | LCC BX8070.L8 L89 2019 (print) | DDC
 238/.41--dc23
LC record available at https://lccn.loc.gov/2018036647

1 2 3 4 5 6 7 8 9 10   29 28 27 26 25 24 23 22 21 20 19

Contents

Abbreviations

AE   American Edition of Luther's Works
LC   Large Catechism
LSB   *Lutheran Service Book*
SC   Small Catechism
WLS   *What Luther Says*

Citation Examples

AE 44:68–69   (American Edition of Luther's Works, volume 44, pages 68–69)
LC I 128–30   (Large Catechism, Part 1, paragraphs 128–30)
WLS § 1044   (*What Luther Says*, paragraph 1044)
SC, Question 15   (*Luther's Small Catechism with Explanation*, Question 15)

Why the Catechism in Our Daily Lives?

〜◦⟨◦〜〜◦⟩◦〜

Blessed is the man who walks not in the counsel of the
wicked, nor stands in the way of sinners, nor sits in the seat
of scoffers; but his delight is in the law of the LORD, and on
His law he meditates day and night. (Psalm 1:1–2)

LUTHER'S WRITINGS ON THE SMALL CATECHISM

The world has now become very sure of itself. It relies on books
and thinks that if these are read it knows everything. The devil
almost succeeded in getting me, too, to become lazy and secure
and to think: "Here you have the books. If you read them you'll
have the answers." So the fanatics and sacramentarians suppose
that because they have read only one little book they know everything. Against such security I pray the catechism every day like
my little Hans and ask God to keep me in his dear, holy Word,
lest I grow weary of it.

AE 54:163

The Beast Needs Tamed — Philip Rigdon

The Founding Fathers of the United States had the right idea. They understood, both from a thorough study of history and from their personal experience, that there is something fundamentally wrong with human beings. While most people in the world—and even many Christians—ignore this reality, Lutherans understand it to be the sinful nature. People are by nature God's enemies and behave selfishly toward one another. For the Founding Fathers, this meant an inclination to assume and abuse political power. For Christians, it's the persistent temptation to neglect regular worship, reception of the Lord's Supper, and study of God's Word. Consequently, such Christians step away from faith in Jesus Christ and return to one of the world's empty alternatives: atheism or idolatry and trust in one's own works or goodness to earn God's divine favor.

Even though Christians have full forgiveness through faith in Christ, they still retain the sinful nature. Only death or Christ's return will terminate the reality entirely. Until then, as Luther explains, it's vital to avail oneself of the Means of Grace, God's Word and Sacraments, through which the Holy Spirit forgives our sins and fortifies faith in the one true Savior, Jesus Christ. It is in these Means that God's Spirit turns our hearts and minds to the cross and the empty tomb and refreshes our souls with the joyous reality of Jesus' full payment for our sins and the comforting good news of His victory over sin, death, and the power of the devil.

———————— ∘⟋⟍∘ ————————

CLOSING PRAYER: Dear heavenly Father, keep us ever mindful of our need for Your Son, Jesus Christ, lest we turn and embrace the vanity of this world. Through Your Word and Sacraments, daily renew our sinful, burdened souls with the merits of Your Son, Jesus Christ. In Your name we pray. Amen.

The Six Chief Parts

The Ten Commandments • The Creed • The Lord's Prayer
• Holy Baptism • Confession • The Sacrament of the Altar

———— ∞⟨∞⟩∞ ————

I will meditate on Your precepts and fix my eyes on Your ways.
I will delight in Your statutes; I will not forget Your word.
(Psalm 119:15–16)

LUTHER'S WRITINGS ON THE SIX CHIEF PARTS

A person who is so rude and unruly as to be unwilling to learn these things is not to be tolerated. For in these . . . parts, everything that we have in the Scriptures is included in short, plain, and simple terms. For the holy fathers or apostles (whoever first taught these things) have summarized the doctrine, life, wisdom, and art of Christians this way. These parts speak, teach, and are focused on them.

Now, when these . . . parts are understood, a person must also know what to say about our Sacraments, which Christ Himself instituted: Baptism and the holy body and blood of Christ. They should know the texts that Matthew [28:19–20] and Mark [16:15–16] record at the close of their Gospels, when Christ said farewell to His disciples and sent them forth.

LC Short Preface 18–20

The Importance of Parts — James Lamb

"Parts is parts." This phrase came from the commercial war between two fast-food chains in the 1980s. A commercial for the chain offering a "pure white meat" chicken sandwich suggested the competitor's chicken nuggets consisted of various chicken parts. A customer asks, "Which parts?" Then came the now-famous answer: "Parts is parts."

Well, not really! Parts are important. Parts help us understand the quality of the whole. Because they come from Scripture, the Six Chief Parts of the Catechism help us understand and remember God's holy revelation to us. Not only that, but these parts also provide guidance in applying this Word of God to our everyday lives.

"What is right and wrong?" The Ten Commandments give God's answer. "But I've done wrong." Confession enables us to seek mercy. "Where do I find hope?" The Creed tells us what our triune God has done to bring forgiveness and eternal life. "How can I talk to God?" The Lord's Prayer provides simple ways to do so. "Where do I find God?" The Sacraments of Holy Baptism and the Lord's Supper remind us that He finds us. Through simple Means He comes to us by His powerful Word. He makes us His own through the splashing of water. He provides forgiveness, life, and salvation in the very body and blood of Jesus.

Parts are important! The Six Chief Parts help us meditate on God's precepts, fix our eyes on His ways, and delight in and remember His Holy Word.

———◦◦◦◦———

CLOSING PRAYER: Heavenly Father, thank You for using Your servant Martin Luther to illuminate for us in simple ways Your Holy Word. Give us faith to delight in them, memorize them, and use them every day as we honor You and serve our neighbor. In Jesus' name. Amen.

What Are the Ten Commandments?

The Ten Commandments are God's Law, His good and loving will for the lives and well-being of all people. (SC, Question 15)

———— ∞〰∞ ————

Do not think that I have come to abolish the Law or the Prophets; I have not come to abolish them but to fulfill them. For truly, I say to you, until heaven and earth pass away, not an iota, not a dot, will pass from the Law until all is accomplished. (Matthew 5:17–18)

LUTHER'S WRITINGS ON THE TEN COMMANDMENTS

It must be true that whoever knows the Ten Commandments perfectly must know all the Scriptures [Matthew 7:12]. So, in all matters and cases, he can advise, help, comfort, judge, and decide both spiritual and temporal matters. Such a person must be qualified to sit in judgment over all doctrines, estates, spirits, laws, and whatever else is in the world [1 Corinthians 6:2–3]. And what, indeed, is the entire Book of Psalms but thoughts and exercises upon the First Commandment? Now I truly know that such lazy "bellies" and arrogant spirits do not understand a single psalm, much less the entire Holy Scriptures. Yet they pretend to know and despise the catechism, which is a short and brief summary of all the Holy Scriptures.

LC Preface 17–18

Confronted by God, Conformed to Christ — Jonathan Rusnak

Some people refuse to darken the doctor's door. "I'll be fine," they say. They're not wrong to be afraid. Crossing that threshold has consequences. No more autonomy. Inspection. Diagnosis.

The Ten Commandments are the doorway. God, the Creator, stands just inside. His design and desire are simple: faith toward Him and love toward others.

You're on the examination table now. The Physician takes a good look. Your defiant disobedience has distorted His design and desire. You're not just sick; you're dying. No, worse! You've suffocated under your own self-obsession.

There is another who calls Himself the door, God's Word made flesh, the obedient Son of the Creator, Jesus. He fulfilled His Father's demands: perfect faith and perfect love. He took your sickness and died your death. Then He burst the door of the tomb and left all your disobedience buried forever. He exited there in order to enter your dead soul by His Holy Spirit. His Spirit now breathes new life into your dry bones in conformity to Himself (Galatians 4:19).

You very well may fear this Great Physician. But He teaches you to love and trust Him. He, and He alone, is your God.

There is one more doorway, though. Jesus stands behind it. The Law still stands as well. But you have already died and are "hidden with Christ" (Colossians 3:3). On the day you cross that threshold, "He who began a good work in you will bring it to completion" (Philippians 1:6), and you will see Him face-to-face.

———— ∞⧸∞◦ ————

CLOSING PRAYER: Dear Creator God, Your Law confronts me. I have distorted Your design and desire. Thank You for Your obedient Son, who saves me from sin, death, and hell. Send Your Spirit to conform me to Christ, according to Your good pleasure, and bring to completion what You have begun in me. Amen.

The First Commandment

You shall have no other gods.

What does this mean? We should fear, love, and trust in God above all things.

⊸○◅◓▻○⊷

You shall love the LORD your God with all your heart and with all your soul and with all your might. (Deuteronomy 6:5)

LUTHER'S WRITINGS ON THE FIRST COMMANDMENT

So everyone made his god that interest to which his heart was inclined. So even in the mind of the heathen to have a god means to trust and believe. But their error is this: their trust is false and wrong. For their trust is not placed in the only God, beside whom there is truly no God in heaven or upon earth [Isaiah 44:6]. Therefore, the heathen really make their self-invented notions and dreams of God an idol. Ultimately, they put their trust in that which is nothing. So it is with all idolatry. For it happens not merely by erecting an image and worshiping it, but rather it happens in the heart. For the heart stands gaping at something else. It seeks help and consolation from creatures, saints, or devils. It neither cares for God, nor looks to Him for anything better than to believe that He is willing to help. The heart does not believe that whatever good it experiences comes from God [James 1:17].

LC I 18–21

What Are We Leaning Into? — Heidi Goehmann

My husband loves bow hunting. He loves it so much that he began setting boundaries for himself on how much time he spent in the woods, lest our marriage take a deer-season-size hit. I love reading. I love it so much that my children have to pass a hand in between my face and the book in order to get my attention. Some people love making their homes beautiful; some people love work; some people love their ideas or their minds. Luther tells us that our hearts are inclined to one interest or another. We are all leaning into something, making something the most important part of that day, that season, or this life. We can also do this with important relationships: loving our children, our spouse, or our friends so much that it crowds out the space intended for God.

Picture inclination not just as letters on a paper but as an action of the whole body. Whatever it is, we love it so much that we lean toward *it* rather than toward God. We rest our head on its chest; we snuggle up to it so close that we can hear its heartbeat. This type of relationship is reserved only for God. We are invited to incline into Him, to lean into His heart and into His Word, and He overflows what we need for all the rest—time, energy, love, attention, and resources. Our inclination is intended only for One—the One who sacrificed everything, leaning into our world, to save us.

———— ⊸o〄o⊷ ————

CLOSING PRAYER: Dear Savior, it is You we love with our whole selves. It is You we trust, You we praise. When we are tempted to incline our hearts, our minds, and our lives to other things and people, help us to rest in You and know that absolutely everything we cast our affection on comes from Your goodness. In Your name we pray. Amen.

The Second Commandment

You shall not misuse the name of the Lord your God.

What does this mean? We should fear and love God so that we do not curse, swear, use satanic arts, lie, or deceive by His name, but call upon it in every trouble, pray, praise, and give thanks.

———◦◦◦———

Offer to God a sacrifice of thanksgiving, and perform your vows to the Most High, and call upon Me in the day of trouble; I will deliver you, and you shall glorify Me. (Psalm 50:14–15)

LUTHER'S WRITINGS ON THE SECOND COMMANDMENT

Now you understand what it means to take God's name in vain. In sum it means (a) to use His name simply for purposes of falsehood, (b) to assert in God's name something that is not true, or (c) to curse, swear, use spells, and, in short, to practice whatever wickedness one may.

Besides this you must also know how to use God's name rightly. For when He says, "You shall not take the name of the Lord, your God, in vain," He wants us to understand at the same time that His name is to be used properly. For His name has been revealed and given to us so that it may be of constant use and profit. So it is natural to conclude that since this commandment forbids using the holy name for falsehood or wickedness, we are, on the other hand, commanded to use His name for truth and for all good, like when someone takes an oath truthfully when it is needed and it is demanded [Numbers 30:2]. This commandment also applies to right teaching and to calling on His name in trouble or praising and thanking Him in prosperity, and so on.

LC I 62–64

The Creator Has a Name — David Loy

It is a little surprising that the Creator of the cosmos has a name. After all, before creation, God was alone. He had no one to talk to. Yet He does have a name—many names, in fact—I AM; Yahweh; the God of Abraham, Isaac, and Jacob; the Lord. We know these names only because He has revealed them to us. This means He is not a far-off, uncaring God. Rather, He wants us to talk to Him. He wants us to thank Him for all He has given us, and He wants us to call on Him in times of trouble because He loves us and will take care of us.

How shameful it is, then, when we use His name to wish evil on others or lead them astray. And how ungrateful we are when we do not thank Him for His gifts or call on Him when we need help. To know His name and His goodness without talking to Him is just as sinful as using His name to curse or deceive. Let us give thanks, then, that He has revealed to us the only name under heaven by which one may be saved: the name of our Lord Jesus Christ. It is never too late to ask Jesus for help and forgiveness, and "everyone who calls on the name of the LORD shall be saved" (Joel 2:32). That is what faith does: it calls to the Lord for help in the day of trouble.

CLOSING PRAYER: Great Jehovah, almighty God, heavenly Father, we thank and praise You for revealing Your names to us. You do not need our prayers, but we need Your goodness. Move us by Your Spirit to pray, praise, and give thanks daily, and graciously hear our prayers. In Jesus' name. Amen.

The Third Commandment

Remember the Sabbath day by keeping it holy.

What does this mean? We should fear and love GOD so that we do not despise preaching and His Word, but hold it sacred and gladly hear and learn it.

———◦◦◦———

So then, there remains a Sabbath rest for the people of God, for whoever has entered God's rest has also rested from his works as God did from His. (Hebrews 4:9–10)

LUTHER'S WRITINGS ON THE THIRD COMMANDMENT

Let me tell you this, even though you know God's Word perfectly and are already a master in all things: you are daily in the devil's kingdom [Colossians 1:13–14]. He ceases neither day nor night to sneak up on you and to kindle in your heart unbelief and wicked thoughts against these three commandments and all the commandments. Therefore, you must always have God's Word in your heart, upon your lips, and in your ears. But where the heart is idle and the Word does not make a sound, the devil breaks in and has done the damage before we are aware [Matthew 13:24–30]. On the other hand, the Word is so effective that whenever it is seriously contemplated, heard, and used, it is bound never to be without fruit [Isaiah 55:11; Mark 4:20]. It always awakens new understanding, pleasure, and devoutness and produces a pure heart and pure thoughts [Philippians 4:8]. For these words are not lazy or dead, but are creative, living words [Hebrews 4:12].

LC I 100–101

Secure Your Supply — Heather Culli

I'll never forget the first time I flew with my children. Being an experienced traveler, I didn't pay very close attention to the attendant's pre-flight safety speech. I was busy attempting to get my squirmy toddler and curious preschooler buckled in and settled with snacks, pillows, books, and everything else I hoped would make for an easy flight. In the midst of my busyness, a portion of the safety speech caught my attention. "Those traveling with young children, in case of emergency, please secure your oxygen mask before securing your child's." Had I heard correctly? It seemed to defy common sense, until I thought through an emergency scenario. I would need to have a generous supply of oxygen in order to help, protect, and comfort my children. Without it, I'd be struggling at best and completely useless at worst.

We Lutherans are notorious for working tirelessly to build and enlarge God's kingdom here on earth. But does our well-intentioned busyness for God sometimes cause us to miss a portion of His safety speech for us? The devil never rests, but we Christians should. That, too, seems to defy common sense. Luther's directive to "always have God's Word in your heart, upon your lips, and in our ears" (LC I 100) is only accomplished when we heed God's call to Sabbath rest. We are sinners in constant need of a generous supply of His Word to fill our sin-depleted hearts. Only when we are full of God's Word are we able to go out into the world and share what's been poured into us with those in need of God's help, protection, and comfort.

———∞◯◯∞———

CLOSING PRAYER: Dear heavenly Father, please forgive my failure to follow Your call to Sabbath rest. You promise that whenever Your Word is seriously contemplated, heard, and used, it is bound never to be without fruit. Humble my heart to not despise preaching and Your Word, but to gladly hear and learn it. In Jesus' name. Amen.

The Fourth Commandment

Honor your father and your mother.

What does this mean? We should fear and love God so that we do not despise or anger our parents and other authorities, but honor them, serve and obey them, love and cherish them.

———⊰⊱———

Children, obey your parents in the Lord, for this is right. . . . Fathers, do not provoke your children to anger, but bring them up in the discipline and instruction of the Lord. (Ephesians 6:1, 4)

LUTHER'S WRITINGS ON THE FOURTH COMMANDMENT

We grow angry and grumble with impatience, and all the good that we have received throughout our life is wiped out ‹of our memory [Psalm 78:17–31]›. We act the same way toward our parents, and there is no child that understands and considers ‹what the parents have endured while nourishing and fostering him›, unless the Holy Spirit grants him this grace.

God knows very well this perverseness of the world; therefore, He admonishes and urges by commandments that everyone consider what his parents have done for him. Each child will discover that he has from them a body and life. He has been fed and reared when otherwise he would have perished a hundred times in his own filth. Therefore, this is a true and good saying of old and wise people: "To God, to parents, and to teachers we can never offer enough thanks and compensation." The person who thinks about and considers this will give all honor to his parents without force and bear them up on his hands as those through whom God has done him all good [Psalm 91:12].

LC I 128–30

It's an Honorable Life — Scott Rauch

Honoring one's parents and all those in authority over us is meant to help us imitate the honor and love we have for God Almighty. As we recognize all that God gives us in our lives, we praise, thank, serve, and obey Him. We do this as we recognize how much we have through Him.

We then have the opportunity to praise, thank, and lovingly serve and obey those He has given to help us live well in life. The world, Satan, and death work desperately to influence us to dishonor God through sin and selfishness. They work to influence us to dishonor our parents, family members, and all those around us. They want us to believe that the best honor is to honor ourselves over all else. And that leads to guilt and condemnation before God.

So we ask God to forgive us because of Jesus' honorable gift of His life, death, and resurrection. We ask Him to empower us to respect and love those He has called to help us live faithful lives. While being family may be tough in this day and age, it is not impossible with the God of love leading us in our day-to-day living.

⸻

CLOSING PRAYER: Father, we praise and thank You for being our God. As Jesus honored You, may we do so also. As Jesus honored His parents and those in authority around Him, lead us to lovingly do so as well. Help us to be honorable people in life. In Jesus' name we pray. Amen.

The Fifth Commandment

You shall not murder.

What does this mean? We should fear and love God so that we do not hurt or harm our neighbor in his body, but help and support him in every physical need.

⸻⸙⸻

But I say to you that everyone who is angry with his brother will be liable to judgment; whoever insults his brother will be liable to the council; and whoever says, "You fool!" will be liable to the hell of fire. (Matthew 5:22)

LUTHER'S WRITINGS ON THE FIFTH COMMANDMENT

The commandment has this goal, that no one would offend his neighbor because of any evil deed, even though he has fully deserved it. For where murder is forbidden, all cause from which murder may spring is also forbidden. For many people, although they do not kill, curse and utter a wish that would stop a person from running far if it were to strike him on the neck. Now, this urge dwells in everyone by nature. It is common practice that no one is willing to suffer at the hands of another person. Therefore, God wants to remove the root and source by which the heart is embittered against our neighbor. He wants to make us used to keeping this commandment ever in view, always to contemplate ourselves in it as in a mirror [James 1:23–25], to regard the will of God, and to turn over to Him the wrong that we suffer with hearty confidence and by calling on His name. In this way we shall let our enemies rage and be angry, doing what they can. We learn to calm our wrath and to have a patient, gentle heart, especially toward those who give us cause to be angry (i.e., our enemies).

LC I 186–87

Redefining Murder — Faith Spelbring

A pastor asked his seventh-grade confirmation students if they thought they could keep the Ten Commandments. One brave girl replied, "I'm pretty sure I've broken all of them, except number five. I've never killed anyone."

The pastor didn't want to burst her bubble, but he was compelled by Scripture to explain that "murder" doesn't only mean the physical act of ending someone else's life. He shared Jesus' words from the Sermon on the Mount, in which Jesus redefines murder to include anything that could lead to bodily harm or injury. A lively discussion followed as the class named all the ways we "murder" people today—gossip, lying about people so others will be mad at them, getting in fights. Ideas flowed.

God knows very personally what murder is like—both in its broad definition, when Jesus was lied about and crowds were stirred up against Him, and in its literal sense, when He was killed to pay for sins that He did not commit. Our good and gracious Lord wants to protect all of us from experiencing murder in all its forms.

CLOSING PRAYER: Merciful Lord, You were slandered and killed because of our wrong, not Yours. You work to protect us from all things that threaten to harm our body and life. Please keep us from causing such harm and use us as Your agents of peace. In Jesus' name we pray. Amen.

THE TEN COMMANDMENTS

The Sixth Commandment

You shall not commit adultery.

What does this mean? We should fear and love God so that we lead a sexually pure and decent life in what we say and do, and husband and wife love and honor each other.

———◦◦◦◦◦———

Let marriage be held in honor among all, and let the marriage bed be undefiled, for God will judge the sexually immoral and the adulterous. (Hebrews 13:4)

LUTHER'S WRITINGS ON THE SIXTH COMMANDMENT

But among us there is such a shameful mess and the very dregs of all vice and lewdness. Therefore, this commandment is directed against all kinds of unchastity, whatever it may be called. Not only is the outward act of adultery forbidden, but also every kind of cause, motive, and means of adultery. Then the heart, the lips, and the whole body may be chaste and offer no opportunity, help, or persuasion toward inchastity. Not only this, but we must also resist temptation, offer protection, and rescue honor wherever there is danger and need. We must give help and counsel, so as to maintain our neighbor's honor. For whenever you abandon this effort when you could resist unchastity, or whenever you overlook it as if it did not concern you, you are as truly guilty of adultery as the one doing the deed. To speak in the briefest way, this much is required of you: everyone must live chastely himself and help his neighbor do the same. So by this commandment God wishes to build a hedge round about [Job 1:10] and protect every spouse so that no one trespasses against him or her.

LC I 202–5

A Marriage Wall — Jonathan Boehne

Satan accused God of building walls of protection all around Job and his family and household (Job 1:10). According to Satan, that's why Job was so upright. Yet Luther says above that those hedges of protection are exactly what God wants around every husband and wife and around every family. Picture a ten-foot-high invisible fence around every marriage, keeping intruders away, building trust in the family, resisting temptations, ensuring safety for the children.

Some would tell us today that marriage is purely a private matter, that the marriages of others are none of our business. Luther couldn't disagree more. God makes marriage the basic building block and foundation of all society. When husbands and wives separate or divorce, it's not a private matter. It affects parents, children, friends, neighbors, church family, and the whole community. In those difficult cases, God is certainly gracious and merciful and will make "all things work together for good, for those who are called according to His purpose" (Romans 8:28). Yet God and all of us would much prefer to use this Sixth Commandment as a great fortress of protection around every marriage.

None of us can say about marriage and families, "That's not my business." God commands everyone to help and protect. Onward, Christian soldiers! Fight for husbands and wives and children. Send anniversary cards. Offer to babysit. Be informed and active in what the government is doing to protect marriage. Encourage church attendance and family devotions. And let marriage be held in honor by us all.

CLOSING PRAYER: Lord, You protect Christ's Bride, the Church, with Your Word of forgiveness and life. In the same way, guard and keep every husband and wife in faithfulness and love. Build a great hedge around them that You and the blessings You give through marriage would be honored by all. Through Jesus Christ, our Lord. Amen.

The Seventh Commandment

You shall not steal.

What does this mean? We should fear and love God so that we do not take our neighbor's money or possessions, or get them in any dishonest way, but help him to improve and protect his possessions and income.

⟶◦◦⟵

Let the thief no longer steal, but rather let him labor, doing honest work with his own hands, so that he may have something to share with anyone in need. (Ephesians 4:28)

LUTHER'S WRITINGS ON THE SEVENTH COMMANDMENT

This is, in short, the way of the world: whoever can steal and rob openly goes free and secure, unmolested by anyone, and even demands that he be honored. Meanwhile, the little burglars, who have once trespassed, must bear the shame and punishment to make the former thieves appear godly and honorable. But let such open thieves know that in God's sight they are the greatest thieves. He will punish them as they are worthy and deserve.

Now, since this commandment is so far-reaching, as just indicated, it is necessary to teach it well and to explain it to the common people. Do not let them go on in their greed and security. But always place before their eyes God's wrath, and instill the same. . . . Therefore, let everyone know his duty, at the risk of God's displeasure: he must do no harm to his neighbor nor deprive him of profit nor commit any act of unfaithfulness or hatred in any bargain or trade. But he must also faithfully preserve his property for him, secure and promote his advantage. This is especially true when one accepts money, wages, and one's livelihood for such service.

LC I 231–33

Jesus' Labor of Love — Philip Rigdon

The Seventh Commandment, like all of the Commandments, is foremost an offense against the First. To steal from another is to place our desire for something above God Almighty, the giver of all good things. In other words, we worship what we intend to steal. We look for satisfaction and security in the materials of this world rather than in our heavenly Father. This is the most eternally devastating aspect of stealing. So consumed in the anticipated joy of what we believe we must have, we underestimate the value of knowing God through His Son, Jesus Christ. The result is the loss not only of whatever we esteemed so highly as to steal but also of the everlasting life, peace, and joy of God's presence in heaven.

Additionally, stealing leads us away from the ministry of Jesus Christ. Paul explains in Ephesians 4:28 that our labor is intended to produce something valuable for our neighbor in need. Jesus came into the world needing nothing. He set aside the goodness of heaven in order to work for sinners. His entire life on earth was a labor of love, from which His Holy Spirit gives to us. Each day, Jesus resisted temptation and obeyed His Father so that, through faith, we could be counted sinless and perfectly obedient. He suffered and died innocently on the cross, from which we receive full forgiveness. Jesus did indeed work to share with those in need!

--- ∞◦❦◦∞ ---

CLOSING PRAYER: Dear heavenly Father, You bless us with so much in this life. By Your Holy Spirit, protect us from temptation to worship the gifts over the giver. Your Son, Jesus, the greatest gift, worked righteousness and forgiveness that we might enjoy the riches of Your grace. Amen.

The Eighth Commandment

You shall not give false testimony against your neighbor. *What does this mean?* We should fear and love God so that we do not tell lies about our neighbor, betray him, slander him, or hurt his reputation, but defend him, speak well of him, and explain everything in the kindest way.

So also the tongue is a small member, yet it boasts of great things. How great a forest is set ablaze by such a small fire! And the tongue is a fire, a world of unrighteousness. The tongue is set among our members, staining the whole body, setting on fire the entire course of life, and set on fire by hell. (James 3:5–6)

LUTHER'S WRITINGS ON THE EIGHTH COMMANDMENT

Now we have the sum and general understanding of this commandment: Let no one do any harm to his neighbor with the tongue, whether friend or foe. Do not speak evil of him, no matter whether it is true or false, unless it is done by commandment or for his reformation. Let everyone use his tongue and make it serve for the best of everyone else, to cover up his neighbor's sins and infirmities [1 Peter 4:8], excuse them, conceal and garnish them with his own reputation. The chief reason for this should be the one that Christ declares in the Gospel, where He includes all commandments about our neighbor, "whatever you wish that others would do to you, do also to them" [Matthew 7:12].

LC I 285–86

The Fire of Tongues — James Lamb

Stories abound of forest fires destroying thousands of acres. Investigation often finds the cause to be a spark from a campfire or a cigarette. James knew of great blazes coming from small fires (James 3:5–6). He knew how similar our tiny tongue is in causing raging havoc for our neighbor. Have you started any such "fires"? Have you said untrue things about others? Have you said true things about others with intent to harm? Take some time to reflect, to repent, and then to rejoice in God's forgiveness.

Now start some good fires! Firefighters sometimes use fire in a controlled burn to eliminate fuel from the approaching flames. This creates a barrier to further damage. Our tongues can prevent further damage when the latest rumor reaches our ears. "I don't think we should be spreading this around." Our tongues can prevent further damage by a positive word. "Well, I don't know about that, but . . ." and then say something good about the person. Our tongues can prevent further damage by following that Golden Rule of Jesus. "How would we like it if such things were said about us?"

Speaking of Jesus, we can learn from Him. "He committed no sin, neither was deceit found in His mouth" (1 Peter 2:22). Speaking of Jesus, His tongue was silent before His accusers so He could win forgiveness for the sins of our tongues (Mark 14:61). He forgives the destructive fires our tongues start. He moves us to "speak well" and start good fires.

CLOSING PRAYER: Dear Jesus, we confess the many sins of our tongue. Forgive us. Give us tongues like Yours, free of deceit and filled with healing. Use us to start "good fires" for the benefit of our neighbor and the extension of Your kingdom. Amen.

The Ninth and Tenth Commandments

You shall not covet your neighbor's house.
What does this mean? We should fear and love God so that we do not scheme to get our neighbor's inheritance or house, or get it in a way which only appears right, but help and be of service to him in keeping it.

You shall not covet your neighbor's wife, or his manservant or maidservant, his ox or donkey, or anything that belongs to your neighbor.
What does this mean? We should fear and love God so that we do not entice or force away our neighbor's wife, workers, or animals, or turn them against him, but urge them to stay and do their duty.

———◦⟨∞⟩◦———

Because of the iniquity of his unjust gain I was angry, I struck him; I hid My face and was angry, but he went on backsliding in the way of his own heart. (Isaiah 57:17)

LUTHER'S WRITINGS ON THE NINTH AND TENTH COMMANDMENTS

In whatever way such things happen, we must know that God does not want you to deprive your neighbor of anything that belongs to him, so that he suffer the loss and you gratify your greed with it. This is true even if you could keep it honorably before the world. For it is a secret and sly trick done "under the hat," as we say, so it may not be noticed. Although you go your way as if you had done no one any wrong, you have still injured your neighbor. If it is not called stealing and cheating, it is still called coveting your neighbor's property, that is, aiming at possession of it, luring it away from him without his consent, and being unwilling to see him enjoy what God has granted him. Even though the judge and everyone must let you keep it, God will not let you keep it. For He sees the deceitful heart and world's malice, which is sure to take an extra long measure wherever you yield to her a finger's breadth. Eventually public wrong and violence follow.

LC I 307–8

Content in Christ — Jonathan Rusnak

They say, "You can't take it with you." I can't argue with that. I can get what I can in the meantime though. Who else will look out for me and my household?

God sees through my self-justifications. I cannot hide, even within my own dark house. Through these commandments, He slips in and flips the switch that shows my greedy, self-reliant, discontented soul. He dissects "the thoughts and intentions of the heart" (Hebrews 4:12).

I see God's provision, but my body and soul are insatiable. I refuse to rely on God to give enough. I cannot stand to see my neighbor have more or better things than me. I imagine ways to feel content for a moment. But God has assured me it won't last (Ecclesiastes 1:2; Romans 8:20).

When I consider Christ, I see someone unpreoccupied with a home in this world (Luke 9:58). He relied on the Creator with eyes wide open to the needs of His neighbors—to my needs. He was content with the "house not made with [human] hands, eternal in the heavens" (2 Corinthians 5:1).

Made new in Him, I have eyes to see that I belong to the household of faith as a living stone within God's eternal Church (Psalm 51:10; Galatians 6:10; 1 Peter 2:4–5). I have eyes to see God's gifts to me and my neighbors. I have contentment in Jesus, God's free gift and my priceless treasure. Through Him, I have a place in the Father's house (John 14:1–3).

⸻ ∽◦◯◦∾ ⸻

CLOSING PRAYER: Dear heavenly Father, You are the giver of all good gifts. Still, my soul is restless and discontent. I seek my own satisfaction. I rely on my own resources. Forgive me. Lead me in faith and love. Open my eyes to Your eternal gifts, to Christ, and to my neighbors. In Your name we pray. Amen.

The Close of the Commandments

What does God say about all these commandments? He says: "I, the LORD your God, am a jealous God, punishing the children for the sin of the fathers to the third and the fourth generation of those who hate Me, but showing love to a thousand generations of those who love Me and keep My commandments." (Ex. 20:5–6)

What does this mean? God threatens to punish all who break these commandments. Therefore, we should fear His wrath and not do anything against them. But He promises grace and every blessing to all who keep these commandments. Therefore, we should also love and trust in Him and gladly do what He commands.

———◦◦◦———

His delight is not in the strength of the horse, nor His pleasure in the legs of a man, but the LORD takes pleasure in those who fear Him, in those who hope in His steadfast love. (Psalm 147:10–11)

LUTHER'S WRITINGS ON THE CLOSE OF THE COMMANDMENTS

Now, there is included in these words (as said before) both an angry, threatening word and a friendly promise. These are to terrify and warn us. They are also to lead and encourage us to receive and highly value His Word as a matter of divine sincerity. For God Himself declares how much He is concerned about it and how rigidly He will enforce it: He will horribly and terribly punish all who despise and transgress His commandments. Also, He declares how richly He will reward, bless, and do all good to those who hold them in high value and gladly do and live according to them. So God demands that all our works proceed from a heart that fears and regards God alone. From such fear the heart avoids everything that is contrary to His will, lest it should move Him to wrath. And, on the other hand, the heart also trusts in Him alone and from love for Him does all He wants. For He speaks to us as friendly as a father and offers us all grace and every good.

LC I 322–23

Two Sides to Every Fear — Heidi Goehmann

Fear is a word most of us would like to obliterate from the Bible. It is easy to believe that it has no place because of our grace-based vantage point in Christ Jesus. Luther helps us to understand the proper place of fear in this writing addressing the Close of the Commandments. Like everything else that is both overtly theological and also experienced tangibly in some way in our daily world and lives, fear is best understood from a Law-and-Gospel perspective. We wouldn't really like dessert with no dinner; we'd be left hungry ten minutes later. And we wouldn't really like a life with no dessert either; then we would miss the sweetness gifted to us by God. Like dessert, fear has two sides. Fear creates images that are uncomfortable for us. However, throwing it off all together, removing it from our experiences, would leave us with less intimacy with God, less understanding of His holiness, His omniscience, and His richness.

God is big. God is perfect. God is jealous. He fills all time and space. I do not want to remove the sweetness of all of this by obliterating the fear included in these attributes. Instead, I embrace the reality of a great, big, powerful God over the universe through the Gospel truth of His plans and purposes in sending Jesus Christ, His dear Son, as my Savior and Redeemer. Jesus stands as Advocate for me. I see God through a Jesus lens. I see even fear through Christ alone.

CLOSING PRAYER: Dear Father in heaven, You are a mighty and perfect God. You also are compassion, love, mercy, and grace in Christ Jesus. Thank You for the saving work of Christ in my life and the way His love changes the shape of fear in my heart. In Jesus' name. Amen.

What is the Creed?

The Creed summarizes all of God's work in creation and human history as taught in the Bible. (SC, Question 104)

—◦◦◦◦◦◦—

May [you] have strength to comprehend with all the saints what is the breadth and length and height and depth, and to know the love of Christ that surpasses knowledge, that you may be filled with all the fullness of God. (Ephesians 3:18–19)

LUTHER'S WRITINGS ON THE APOSTLES' CREED

To create and preserve all things, to make satisfaction for sin, to forgive sins, to raise from the dead, and to give eternal life are works of the whole Divine Majesty. Yet the Father is especially revealed in the work of creation, which proceeds originally from Him, as the first Person; the Son in the work of redemption, which He performed in His own Person; the Holy Ghost in the work of sanctification, for which He in particular is sent and in which He reveals Himself. These distinctions are made that Christians may have the simple and certain assurance of the existence of only one God and yet three Persons in the one Divine Essence. These are truths which the pious fathers have diligently gathered from the writings of Moses, the prophets, and the apostles and have maintained against all heretics.

This faith has come down to us as an inheritance, and until the present day God has maintained it with power in His church against all sects and devils. Therefore we must abide by it in simplicity and not be wise in our own conceit; for Christians are expected to believe things that seem foolish to reason.

WLS § 1044

You Believe in God, but Which One? — David Loy

Our God is no generic, least-common-denominator deity. Ours is a very particular God who did particular deeds for a particular reason. He created us from dust and His own breath. He redeemed us through the blood of His Son, Jesus. He pours out His Spirit on us to make us members of His household and heirs of eternal life. All this He does because He loves us with a love that is both undying as eternity and dies to give us life. His love and His deeds distinguish Him from every pretender to His throne, and they give us an eternal place around His throne.

It is therefore vitally important that we be very clear who our God is. Saying, "I believe in God," is not specific enough. Many non-Christians say the very same thing. The Apostles' Creed helps us get specific. We believe in one God—Father, Son, and Holy Spirit. We believe in the God who created all things, the Father of our Lord Jesus Christ. We believe in His only Son, our Lord, who gave His life to redeem us from sin, death, and the devil and who rose in glory on the third day. We believe in the Holy Spirit, whose divine power creates faith where there was none and warms our cold hearts. When we confess the Creed, we confess this God in all His uniqueness. It is this God alone whom we confess, because it is this God alone who saves.

———⋙⋘———

CLOSING PRAYER: Gracious Father, give us a clear confession of faith in Jesus by the power of Your Holy Spirit, so that we may rejoice eternally in the salvation You have prepared for us and boldly tell others the good news of Your love in Christ. In His name we pray. Amen.

What Does the Word *Trinity* Mean?

It means three in one. The Church has used the word *Trinity* to maintain the Bible's witness that the Father, Son, and Spirit are three distinct persons and yet are one God. This is the greatest mystery of the Christian faith. (SC, Question 110)

For in Him [Christ] the whole fullness of deity dwells bodily, and you have been filled in Him, who is the head of all rule and authority. (Colossians 2:9–10)

LUTHER'S WRITINGS ON THE TRINITY

We should stay with the true, ancient belief that there are three distinct Persons—Father, Son, and Holy Ghost—in the eternal Godhead. This is the most sublime and the first article of Christian faith. . . . We call it the article of the Holy Divine Threeness. But to say that God is threefold is very poor language, for in the Godhead the highest Oneness exists. Some speak of a Threeness *(Dreiheit)*, but this expression is ridiculous. Augustine, too, complains that he has no fitting word for the mystery. I may not say that there are three gods as there are three men or three angels. Rather I must say that there is only one eternal God. To be sure, a threeness does exist in the Godhead, but this threeness exists in the Persons of the one Godhead. Not three Gods, not three Lords, not three Creators, but one God, one Lord, one Creator, or, as we are wont to say: One divine Essence and yet three distinct Persons—Father, Son, and Holy Ghost. I call this Being a Threeness *(ein Gedrittes)*, for threefoldness sounds strange. I cannot give this Being a fitting name.

WLS § 4450

Fuzzy Math — Heather Culli

During the 2000 presidential election, the phrase "fuzzy math" entered the national vocabulary. It was used by politicians to attack opponents' positions based on numbers that just didn't seem to add up. At first glance, the Holy Trinity seems to be a good example of fuzzy math. How can 1 Father + 1 Son +1 Holy Spirit = 1 God? It doesn't add up. Even great minds like St. Augustine and Luther failed in their attempts to do the math!

Unlike politicians who use numbers to cloak, conceal, and confuse, God uses this complex equation to unveil, uncover, and unravel one of the great mysteries of Christian doctrine. Scripture is filled with passages detailing the existence and distinct role of each person of the Trinity. God the Father is the beginning and end of all creation. God the Son comes to earth as a human being to be sacrificed and resurrected for our salvation. God the Holy Spirit dwells with believers on earth to grow and sustain faith. The equation becomes fuzzy when we factor in Scripture's mention of there being only one God. Yet even in this seeming contradiction, God unveils His divine nature. He is not a finite being ruled by earthly constraints. Through our struggle to accept what we can't understand, God exposes and uncovers the root cause of sin that Satan recognizes and regularly exploits. We human beings want to be equal to God. The mystery of the Holy Trinity brings us humbly to our knees to confront and confess our own weakness. It turns our eyes to the kingdom of God, where we know all mysteries will one day be revealed.

$\infty\!\!\infty\!\!\infty\!\!\infty$

CLOSING PRAYER: Dear heavenly Father, our earthly minds cannot possibly comprehend all that You are. Forgive us when our relentless pursuit for understanding clouds our faith. Focus our hearts and minds on Your truth. Help us to simply be still and know that You are God. In Your name we pray. Amen.

The First Article

I believe in God, the Father Almighty, Maker of heaven and earth.

What does this mean? I believe that God has made me and all creatures; that He has given me my body and soul, eyes, ears, and all my members, my reason and all my senses, and still takes care of them. . . .

———∾∘⌾∘∾———

For You formed my inward parts; You knitted me together in my mother's womb. I praise You, for I am fearfully and wonderfully made. Wonderful are Your works; my soul knows it very well. (Psalm 139:13–14)

LUTHER'S WRITINGS ON THE FIRST ARTICLE OF THE APOSTLES' CREED

Here there is no difference between a pregnant cow and a woman with child. But Moses shows that in their first state there was a very great difference, inasmuch as man was created by a unique counsel and wisdom and shaped by the finger of God.

This difference between the origin of man and that of cattle also points to the immortality of the soul, of which we have previously spoken. Although all the remaining works of God are perfect objects of wonder and are very sublime, this nevertheless proves conclusively that man is the most outstanding creature: when God creates him, He takes counsel and employs a new procedure. He does not leave it to the earth to produce him, like the animals and the trees. But He Himself shapes him according to His image as if he were God's partner and one who would enjoy God's rest. And so Adam is a dead and inactive clod before he is formed by the Lord. God takes that clod and forms from it a most beautiful creature which has a share in immortality.

AE 1:83–84

The Great Sand Man Maker — Scott Rauch

He's on His hands and knees, moving the very grains of sand into the curves and forms that would soon change into flesh and bone. He gently caresses with His fingers the muscles, organs, and skin that will allow this man, and ultimately a woman, to move with grace and flair in His creation. He leans over and, into the very nostrils He has carved out, breathes not just physical air that inflates the man's lungs and activates the blood that pulses through the man's body but even His very spirit into this man, and ultimately into that woman. They, the very image of God—Father, Son, and Holy Spirit—will imitate their Creator in love and power.

He gives us all that we need to be the ones who provide care and leadership in His creation. He calls us to follow Him in His creativity and in how He cares. We, the very real modern-day 4-D image of God, are called to serve as co-caretakers in our day and age.

When we sin and cross that line of selfishly believing we don't need God to continue this work, He does not abandon us. When we sin and actively harm or neglect His creation, He enters into it Himself, redeeming us through Jesus. He restores our very body and soul by His grace and gives us faith to once again join Him in His creative and sustaining work. May we in joy follow Him well!

———⊸०ᴄᴆ०⊶———

CLOSING PRAYER: Father, You have created us, body and soul, to be as You are and do as You do. Show us clearly, through Jesus who lives in us by the Holy Spirit's power, how we are to care for Your creation. In Jesus' name. Amen.

The First Article

. . . He also gives me clothing and shoes, food and drink, house and home, wife and children, land, animals, and all I have. He richly and daily provides me with all that I need to support this body and life. . . .

⟶∽◦⟋⟍◦∾⟵

Look at the birds of the air: they neither sow nor reap nor gather into barns, and yet your heavenly Father feeds them. Are you not of more value than they? . . . And why are you anxious about clothing? Consider the lilies of the field, how they grow: they neither toil nor spin, yet I tell you, even Solomon in all his glory was not arrayed like one of these. (Matthew 6:26, 28–29)

LUTHER'S WRITINGS ON THE FIRST ARTICLE OF THE APOSTLES' CREED

He gives me food and drink, clothing and support, wife and children, domestic servants, house and home, and more. Besides, He causes all created things to serve for the uses and necessities of life. These include the sun, moon, and stars in the heavens, day and night, air, fire, water, earth, and whatever it bears and produces. They include birds and fish, beasts, grain, and all kinds of produce [Psalm 104]. They also include whatever else there is for bodily and temporal goods, like good government, peace, and security. So we learn from this article that none of us owns for himself, nor can preserve, his life nor anything that is here listed or can be listed. This is true no matter how small and unimportant a thing it might be. For all is included in the word *Creator*.

LC II 13–16

The Ma'am with Sad Ham — Faith Spelbring

Easter morning, a mother and her daughters dressed up and walked to church. It was snowing when they returned, but the girls didn't mind the cold. The Easter lilies and story of Jesus' resurrection were all they could think about. When they reached their house, they found a white package on their step. Inside the package was a ham. The girls were confused. Ham seemed like a silly thing to find on the step. The mother began to cry. Her young girls asked why ham made her sad. She explained, "I'm crying because our God is so good. I had nothing to serve for dinner, but God provided exactly what we needed."

Like the birds of the air, the young girls weren't anxious about what they would eat, but their mom did worry. She knew it was her job to feed her family, but she didn't have the resources to do it herself. What she did have was a God who provides and did so that day through the generosity of a neighbor.

This true story is only one example of God's amazing care for His creation. The Lord gives us what we need, whether that be food for our tables, roofs over our heads, or a friend's text on a bad day. We are tempted to worry about life, but God, who made heaven and earth, listens to our every cry and sustains us and all creation. Through times of abundance or scarcity, chaos or peace, He gives us what we need.

∽⚬⚬∼

CLOSING PRAYER: Thanks and praise to You, heavenly Father, for providing all we need to sustain this body and life! Give us strength to trust You with whatever would cause us to worry. Use us in Your work of caring for others. In the name of Your Son, Jesus, we pray. Amen.

The First Article

. . . He defends me against all danger and
guards and protects me from all evil. . . .

———∞◦◯◦∞———

My help comes from the LORD, who made heaven
and earth. . . . The LORD will keep you from all evil;
He will keep your life. (Psalm 121:2, 7)

LUTHER'S WRITINGS ON THE FIRST ARTICLE OF THE APOSTLES' CREED

If none of these evils befalls us, we should consider this a gain and
no small comfort in the evil that does in fact become our lot, and
exclaim with Jeremiah, "It is of the Lord's mercies that we are not
consumed" [Lam. 3:22]. When none of these things happens to
us it is because the preventing right hand of the Most High surrounds us on all sides with great might and like a wall (as is seen in
the case of Job), so that Satan and the evils in their frustration can
only be grievously vexed. From this we see how dearly we should
love God whenever some evil afflicts us, for by that one evil our
most loving Father would want us to see how many evils would
threaten and attack us if he himself did not stand in the way. It is
as if he said, "Satan and a host of evils desire you that they may
sift you as wheat [Luke 22:31], but I have been able to limit the
sea and to say to it, 'To this place shall you come and here shall
your proud waves be stayed,'" as he says in Job 38 [:11].

AE 42:128–29

Our Most Loving Father — Jonathan Boehne

God governs all the seas. In the beginning, He told the waves where they would halt (Job 38:11). On the boat with His disciples, Jesus told the water to be still. But what about hurricanes and tsunamis? Why does God occasionally allow the sea to go past its bounds? According to Luther, God does it because He loves us! He lets the sea escape once in a while to remind us that He is governor.

What a strange way to look at evils! When some little evil attacks us, Luther says we should "dearly . . . love God" for it. That's not our usual play. We often take evil as an occasion to question God or become angry with Him. Certainly there is a time to voice our complaint to God, as many saints do in the Scriptures. Yet an evil may just as well be our reminder to give thanks and praise to God for His otherwise vigilant defense.

If God were not governor of all things, where would we be? Just how many evils would Satan attack us with if God were not attending to us with His holy angels? Sufferings will most certainly come. But when they do, we'll remember how small they are compared to the daily blessings God sends. The worst evil, death, has already been told to halt its "proud waves" (Job 38:11) by Jesus' resurrection from the dead. We can trust Him to defend and guard us in every other evil.

⸺⬦⬦⬦⸺

CLOSING PRAYER: Merciful Lord, our help comes from You, who made heaven and earth. In every suffering, direct us to Your dear love and to all the blessings You give us in Jesus Christ. Govern us in body and soul that we may finally be delivered from all evil. Through Jesus Christ, our Lord. Amen.

The First Article

... All this He does only out of fatherly, divine goodness and mercy, without any merit or worthiness in me. For all this it is my duty to thank and praise, serve and obey Him.

∞∘⟳∘∞

For everything created by God is good, and nothing is to be rejected if it is received with thanksgiving, for it is made holy by the word of God and prayer. (1 Timothy 4:4–5)

Luther's Writings on the First Article of the Apostles' Creed

"What sacrifice will you bring to me? Do I eat the flesh of bulls or drink the blood of goats? For the world is mine, all the birds of the air and every beast of the field, every offering you can render is continually before me. Offer to your God a sacrifice of praise and pay him the vows you have made. The sacrifice of praise honors me duly and that is the way to salvation." These texts clearly show that it must be a sacrifice of praise and thanksgiving, in order to be acceptable to God, certainly never an offering without praise and thanksgiving. If offered without praise and thanksgiving, he dislikes it and will not accept it, as he says, Isaiah 1[:11]: "What to me is your sacrifice? I have enough of your burnt offerings," etc.

There is nothing else we can give God, for he possesses everything and what we own, we have from him. We can give him nothing but praise and thanksgiving and honor. . . . Praise is simply confessing the good gifts which we have received from God, not ascribing them to ourselves but to him alone, and returning them to him.

AE 52:276–77

God Would Know Us and Be Close — Philip Rigdon

So much of the Christian life is bound up in setting aside the self and letting God be good. As Luther explains here, it is arrogant presumption to claim as ours what belongs to God alone. What vanity to believe that God needs what we can offer! Such thinking is rooted in pride and fear—I will share what I have and God will regard me favorably. Or if I do not give to God, He will withdraw His blessings or punish me. Even the praise God expects in response to His blessings is for our good. Gratitude reminds us of the giver. The practice of thanksgiving and praise is communication with the heavenly Father. Both fill the human heart with joy and deprive it of fear.

God's wish for communication reflects His larger desire—to know and have intimacy with sinners. When I recognize God's benevolence, I learn what He is like. When I share what God has given with those in need, I further grasp what Jesus did for me. As Paul explains in 1 Timothy 4, Christian prayer and praise are not holy by themselves; they are made so in the blood of Jesus Christ. God accepts my prayer and praise through faith in His Son. God sent Jesus so that He could know sinners and restore the intimacy our disobedience destroyed in the Garden of Eden. Through faith in Jesus, we receive not merely clothing, food, house, and home, but the unchangeable love of the Father and everlasting sonship in His house.

CLOSING PRAYER: Dear Father, we fail to trust in Your goodness because of our sin and tragic experience in this world. Remove our vain hearts and calm our fears, that we would accept Your grace as it is, out of divine goodness and mercy, through Jesus Christ. Amen.

The Second Article

And [I believe] in Jesus Christ, His only Son, our Lord, who was conceived by the Holy Spirit, born of the Virgin Mary, suffered under Pontius Pilate, was crucified, died and was buried. He descended into hell. The third day He rose again from the dead. He ascended into heaven and sits at the right hand of God, the Father Almighty. From thence He will come to judge the living and the dead.

What does this mean? I believe that Jesus Christ, true God, begotten of the Father from eternity, and also true man, born of the Virgin Mary, is my Lord. . . .

⚬⚬⚬⚬⚬

And the angel answered her, "The Holy Spirit will come upon you, and the power of the Most High will overshadow you; therefore the child to be born will be called holy—the Son of God." (Luke 1:35)

LUTHER'S WRITINGS ON THE SECOND ARTICLE OF THE APOSTLES' CREED

Indeed, who could ever grasp [the full meaning of] these words of the evangelist: "a Savior, who is the Lord," and, "to you"! I know well enough how to talk about it and what to believe about it, just as others do. So there are many who have this belief and do not doubt this first belief that Christ is the Lord, the Savior, and the virgin's Son. This I too have never doubted. But if these words are planted no higher than in my thoughts, then they have no firm roots. We are certain that this was proclaimed by the angel, but the firm faith does not follow. For the reason does not understand both sides of this faith, first that Christ is a man, but also the Savior and Lord or King. This needs to be revealed from heaven. One who really has the first faith also has the other. . . . Beyond the first faith there must be the second faith, that Christ is not only the virgin's Son, but also the Lord of angels and the Savior of men.

AE 51:212–13

The Mysterious and Mundane — James Lamb

Like all of us, Jesus had a birthday. It was less sanitary, but much like ours. With pain and pushing, Mary gave birth to Jesus, a tiny human, true man. Like all of us, Jesus had a lifeday, the day He began to grow in Mary's womb. But it cannot compare to ours at all! Jesus' life began through the power of the most high God! A tiny speck in Mary's womb was deemed "the Son of God."

Jesus was true man and true God. The true man part we get. The true God part falls outside of our reason. That He was both at the same time moves us into the mysterious.

But God loves a mystery! He loves to reveal mysteries through faith. Through faith, we get it. Through faith, we understand the need for both the mystery of Jesus' lifeday and the mundane of His birthday. Because of both, God gives us a new lifeday!

Baptism unites us with Jesus' death and resurrection. As true man, He could die. As true God, His death pays sufficient ransom for sin. As true God, He could rise again and bring us with Him to new life, now and eternally.

When you celebrate your birthday, remember that Jesus had one too. He was true man. But also celebrate your lifeday (think back about nine months from your birthday!). Remember that Jesus had one too, but much different from yours. He was true God. Then, celebrate your new lifeday, made possible through the mundane and mysterious.

CLOSING PRAYER: Lord Jesus, true man and true God, forgive my overuse of reason when it comes to understanding Your divine and human natures. Give me faith to trust in what You have revealed through Your Word. Help me live in gratitude for this revelation. In Your name. Amen.

The Second Article

. . . who has redeemed me, a lost and condemned person, purchased and won me from all sins, from death, and from the power of the devil; not with gold or silver, but with His holy, precious blood and with His innocent suffering and death. . . .

———⬥◦⬥◦⬥———

And if you call on Him as Father who judges impartially according to each one's deeds, conduct yourselves with fear throughout the time of your exile, knowing that you were ransomed from the futile ways inherited from your forefathers, not with perishable things such as silver or gold, but with the precious blood of Christ, like that of a lamb without blemish or spot. (1 Peter 1:17–19)

LUTHER'S WRITINGS ON THE SECOND ARTICLE OF THE APOSTLES' CREED

But the devil did not permit man the honor and fortune of being God's child and heir, and he cast him into sin, and through his disobedience caused all of us after the fall to be reckoned as disobedient so that we are neither God's children nor His heirs. . . . So thoroughly have we been corrupted by sin.

Then comes Jesus Christ, God's Son, and lifts up the creatures that the devil had destroyed through sin and sets them right again. Through sin, the devil had captured us. We were neither God's children nor heirs. But here it says that we should return again to the former honor of being God's children and recipients of everlasting life. This is what Scripture teaches: Jesus Christ, God's Son, accomplished this, not with gold or silver [1 Pet. 1:18], not with gun or sword. No, rather, He gave up His own body, and He is true God, conceived by the Holy Spirit, and was a human being born of the Virgin Mary, etc.

AE 57:247–48

Jesus' Blood for You — Jonathan Rusnak

The heart of the catechism is the Creed. The heart of the Creed is Christ. The heart of Christ pumps blood. It isn't metaphor or mere idea but vivid reality. Here, God calls you to set your heart on His and to boldly believe that Jesus' blood is for you.

Why does Jesus shed His blood? He wants you, and that's the price (Hebrews 9:22). You were lost and condemned. You deserved only what you had earned: the wages of sin, sin that rejects God and hoards silver and gold as if life depends on it. And yet, your sin and your price did not stop Him.

The limitless one limited Himself to a human body with flesh and blood so that He could spend that flesh and blood on *you* (Colossians 1:19–20; Hebrews 2:14). He willingly redeemed you by His blood (Hebrews 9:12). Your Redeemer loves you with an everlasting love (Isaiah 54:8). His blood now flows from His cross to you through water, bread, and wine, delivering forgiveness, life, and salvation to you and for you (Hebrews 10:19; 12:24).

This is the central article of the Christian faith. It defies all rational explanation. From God's heart, the blood of Jesus flows. He invites you to believe it's for you. This central truth bleeds onto every other page of the catechism. It flows, transfused, through your veins as well, giving you His eternal life.

What else is there for you to do but set your heart on Him?

———————— ∞◦◯◯◦∞ ————————

CLOSING PRAYER: "Glory be to Jesus, Who in bitter pains Poured for me the lifeblood From His sacred veins! Grace and life eternal In that blood I find; Blest be His compassion, Infinitely kind! . . . Lift we, then, our voices, Swell the mighty flood; Louder still and louder Praise the precious blood!" (*LSB* 433:1–2, 6). Amen.

The Second Article

. . . that I may be His own and live under Him in His kingdom and serve Him in everlasting righteousness, innocence, and blessedness. . . .

———— ∞◦◯◦∞ ————

But seek first the kingdom of God and His righteousness, and all these things will be added to you. (Matthew 6:33)

LUTHER'S WRITINGS ON THE SECOND ARTICLE OF THE APOSTLES' CREED

What the kingdom of God is has often been stated. To put it most briefly, it does not mean outward things like eating and drinking (Rom. 14:17) nor other works that we can do. Rather, it means believing in Jesus Christ. In this kingdom He is the Head and the only King, in whom and through whom we have everything; whoever abides in it cannot be harmed by any sin, death, or misfortune, but has eternal life, joy, and salvation. Here he begins in this faith, but on the Last Day all will be revealed, and he will be eternally perfected in it.

Now, what does it mean to "seek" this kingdom? What is the method of reaching it, and what way or path leads to it? . . . For there are many ways, but they are all departures from that one way of believing in Christ and practicing and applying the Gospel, to which faith clings. This involves growing and being strengthened at heart through preaching, listening, reading, singing, meditating, and every other possible way. And it involves blossoming out in fruits, to advance it and to lead many other people to it.

AE 21:204

God's Kingdom Come to My Day — Heidi Goehmann

God's kingdom sounds like a place we all want to live in. Innocence, blessedness, and righteousness sound far better than pain, suffering, and struggle. However, on every morning we rise up and every day we walk out our door, we are quickly reminded that it's not a simple either/or. Luther calls to our attention that we cannot be harmed by sin, death, or misfortune, but he never promises that they won't come to us within God's kingdom. Rather, we do rise up and walk out that door each day armed with the promises of God—armed with eternal life, joy, and salvation in Jesus Christ, Lord of all, master of our every day.

We "seek first the kingdom of God" every time we open our Bible, every time the Holy Spirit brings Him to mind, every time we breathe a prayer of help or praise. All these things, alongside gathering with the Body of Christ, singing His praise, and taking His Supper, give us strength to cling tight to the promise that "I may be His own" and walk with that promise into each day. Without this promise, we shrivel, we shrink back, we feel defeated before the day dawns. But with it, with "I am His own" on our souls, we are the warriors, the scribes, the laborers, and the carriers of hope for His kingdom everywhere we go. His kingdom is not found in our works, but we certainly bring His kingdom to all the work we touch by bearing His name.

―∞◌∞―

CLOSING PRAYER: Father, You seek us first and call us Your own. Therefore, we rest in this identity as believers, workers, spouses, parents, members of the Church, and citizens in this world. We wait for Your return with perseverance, inviting You actively into our days. In Jesus Christ we pray. Amen.

The Second Article

... just as He is risen from the dead, lives and reigns to all eternity.

⊸○⬤○⬤○⊸

When the perishable puts on the imperishable, and the mortal puts on immortality, then shall come to pass the saying that is written: "Death is swallowed up in victory." (1 Corinthians 15:54)

LUTHER'S WRITINGS ON THE SECOND ARTICLE OF THE APOSTLES' CREED

You cast your sins from yourself onto Christ when you firmly believe that his wounds and sufferings are your sins, to be borne and paid for by him. . . . If we allow sin to remain in our conscience and try to deal with it there, or if we look at sin in our heart, it will be much too strong for us and will live on forever. But if we behold it resting on Christ and [see it] overcome by his resurrection, and then boldly believe this, even it is dead and nullified. Sin cannot remain on Christ, since it is swallowed up by his resurrection. Now you see no wounds, no pain in him, and no sign of sin. Thus St. Paul declares that "Christ died for our sin and rose for our justification" [Rom. 4:25]. That is to say, in his suffering Christ makes our sin known and thus destroys it, but through his resurrection he justifies us and delivers us from all sin, if we believe this.

AE 42:12–13

The Linchpin — David Loy

Easter is the linchpin of the New Testament. Christmas without Easter would be just another sentimental story. Good Friday without Easter would be nothing more than a tragic miscarriage of justice. Pentecost without Easter would be just a bizarre event starting off another dubious religion. But Easter gives Christmas, Good Friday, and Pentecost a whole new meaning. It was no ordinary baby who was born to Mary, but rather God in human flesh who came to rescue us from the curse of sin by taking it on Himself. It was no mere political activist whose blood was shed on the cross, but rather the holy and righteous Son of God who shed His innocent blood in place of our guilty blood. His rising from the dead means that no power in heaven or on earth can successfully oppose Him. His Church will flourish—is flourishing—in the power of the Spirit, and the gates of hell cannot withstand it. It will endure forever.

Easter is likewise the linchpin of the story of your life. The God who died for you did not stay dead. He rose from the dead in glory, and no power can successfully oppose Him. When the called and ordained servant of Christ says your sins are forgiven, they really are, because Christ is risen from the dead. When you pray for the Spirit's help in temptation, you receive it, because Christ is risen from the dead. And when your last hour comes and death has done its worst, you will nevertheless live forever, because Christ is risen from the dead.

⊷∘C⧜∘⊶

CLOSING PRAYER: Blessed Lord of Life, strengthen our faith in the resurrection of Jesus Christ from the dead. Teach us to see in His resurrection our own victory over sin, death, and the devil, and when our last hour comes, sustain us in this same faith. In the name of Jesus. Amen.

The Third Article

I believe in the Holy Spirit, the holy Christian church, the communion of saints, the forgiveness of sins, the resurrection of the body, and the life everlasting. Amen.

What does this mean? I believe that I cannot by my own reason or strength believe in Jesus Christ, my Lord, or come to Him; but the Holy Spirit has called me by the Gospel, enlightened me with His gifts, sanctified and kept me in the true faith. . . .

─────────⋘∘⋙─────────

Now we have received not the spirit of the world, but the Spirit who is from God, that we might understand the things freely given us by God. (1 Corinthians 2:12)

LUTHER'S WRITINGS ON THE THIRD ARTICLE OF THE APOSTLES' CREED

The whole world with all diligence has struggled to figure out what God is, what He has in mind and does. Yet the world has never been able to grasp ‹the knowledge and understanding of› any of these things. But here we have everything in richest measure. For here in all three articles God has revealed Himself and opened the deepest abyss of His fatherly heart and His pure, inexpressible love [Ephesians 3:18–19]. He has created us for this very reason, that He might redeem and sanctify us. In addition to giving and imparting to us everything in heaven and upon earth, He has even given to us His Son and the Holy Spirit, who brings us to Himself [Romans 8:14, 32]. For (as explained above) we could never grasp the knowledge of the Father's grace and favor except through the Lord Christ. . . . But we couldn't know anything about Christ either, unless it had been revealed by the Holy Spirit [1 Corinthians 2:12].   LC II 63–65

What Do You Do? — Heather Culli

In Western culture, making small talk is a socially acceptable way for two strangers to get better acquainted with each other. After polite introductions, the conversation usually follows a predictable progression that begins with "Where are you from?" and often ends with a less-than-riveting discussion on the weather. Somewhere in between, one is very likely to ask or be asked the question "What do you do?" Why is this one of the first things we ask a new acquaintance? Because our work defines us, especially as Americans. It is part of our identity.

Each article in the Apostles' Creed follows a similar pattern. Introductions are made, and then a job description is shared, giving the reader insight into the unique identity of each person of the Godhead. It is especially useful here in the Third Article. Answering the question "What do you do?" for God the Father and God the Son is fairly simple for most Christians. God creates. Jesus saves. The Holy Spirit does . . . what? His work is not so easily defined. But a quick glance at His job description reveals that He is the ultimate multitasker! In fact, here is just a small part of the Holy Spirit's to-do list: impart understanding, enlighten, sanctify, keep true to the faith. Where can we see His work in action? For the Father, we need only look to the world He created. For the Son, we need only look to the cross and the open tomb. This article shows us where to look for the work of the Holy Spirit—namely, the Church, its Sacraments, and life eternal. While we will never figure out what God is, this statement of faith brings us to a deeper understanding and can be the beginning of a fascinating conversation.

CLOSING PRAYER: Dear God, no one can grasp the knowledge and understanding of who You are and all You do. Your love for us is boundless. Thank You for creating us, sending Your Son to save us, and empowering the Holy Spirit to create and sustain our faith. All glory, honor, and praise be to You now and forevermore. Amen.

The Third Article

... In the same way He calls, gathers, enlightens, and sanctifies the whole Christian church on earth, and keeps it with Jesus Christ in the one true faith. . . .

⟶∘⟨∾⟩∘⟵

And I have other sheep that are not of this fold.
I must bring them also, and they will listen to
My voice. So there will be one flock, one shepherd.
(John 10:16)

LUTHER'S WRITINGS ON THE THIRD ARTICLE OF THE APOSTLES' CREED

Scripture speaks about Christendom very simply and in only one way. . . . *The first way,* according to Scripture, is that Christendom means an assembly of all the people on earth who believe in Christ, as we pray in the Creed, "I believe in the Holy Spirit, the communion of saints." This community or assembly means all those who live in true faith, hope, and love. Thus the essence, life, and nature of Christendom is not a physical assembly, but an assembly of hearts in one faith, as St. Paul says in Ephesians 4[:5], "One baptism, one faith, one Lord." Accordingly, regardless of whether a thousand miles separates them physically, they are still called one assembly in spirit, as long as each one preaches, believes, hopes, loves, and lives like the other. So we sing about the Holy Spirit, "You have brought many tongues together into the unity of faith." This is what spiritual unity really means, on the basis of which men are called a "communion of saints." This unity alone is sufficient to create Christendom, and without it, no unity—be it that of city, time, persons, work, or whatever else it may be—can create Christendom.

AE 39:65

Going as Church — Scott Rauch

We love to use the phrase "going to church." Even though many times it means we're going to a building or place to worship the Lord, we also understand that it is a place or building that gathers God's people together in the midst of a community that He loves. As we "go to church," we are reminded that we are going to the community that God has bought through the blood of Jesus and brings together every day by the power of the Holy Spirit.

Our heavenly Father invites us to "see" the Church as He sees it. He sees it as His Son's Body through the vision of the Holy Spirit. He sings about the Church, sings through it, and sings out of it into a world that needs to see and hear Him. He speaks to her with bold and tender words. He is intimately, really present in and with her. When we struggle to see ourselves as He does, when we fall short and sin against Him and one another, when we don't represent our faithful God well, He still knows we are His. He will guide us to continue to become who He knows us to be—Jesus' Body, a community alive with the love of Jesus, set apart for the good works He has already prepared for us to do. We faithfully confess this reality even as we daily work to live in it. May we be a community of saints that is always going as the Church.

CLOSING PRAYER: Lord God, we acknowledge You to be the Lord of Your Church. Help us to see ourselves as You do—as the living Body of Christ. Move us to be in the kind of community You saved us to be. Bless us in Jesus. Amen.

The Third Article

... In this Christian church He daily and richly forgives all my sins and the sins of all believers. ...

———⊸∘⟋⟍∘⊸———

My little children, I am writing these things to you so that you may not sin. But if anyone does sin, we have an advocate with the Father, Jesus Christ the righteous. He is the propitiation for our sins, and not for ours only but also for the sins of the whole world. (1 John 2:1–2)

LUTHER'S WRITINGS ON THE THIRD ARTICLE OF THE APOSTLES' CREED

Our holiness does not consist of what we have already achieved. This forgiveness of sins is certainly present, but not yet fully grasped. Thus the resurrection of the flesh is certainly present, but I do not yet see it. Thus eternal life [is certainly present], because He who began it is [present, and where He] is, there is no sin, unholiness, or death in them. ‹Otherwise we are condemned, but we must believe. If we do not feel it, it is nevertheless complete in Christ, who has finished it.› That answers those who say that people ought to sense everything that Christians preach. No, for often it happens that the father or mother of a family, [or] a male or female servant, goes about ‹doing their vocation›, and it is not evident that in this person there is a saint; it is hidden even from them. For you do not see Christ, and as little [do you see] my holiness, even though I am holy in Him. In addition I have the signs of Baptism and the Eucharist.

AE 57:5 (brackets from original)

Finished Forgiveness — Faith Spelbring

A student stopped by his campus church between classes and asked to meet with both the pastor and the director of Christian education for confession. He confessed the same sin he had confessed the week before. He simply couldn't shake the feelings of regret. He said he didn't feel like God had forgiven him.

The campus pastor reminded the young student that God's forgiveness was a sure thing, adding, "People have a more difficult time forgiving than God does. We seem to lay our burdens at the foot of the cross, only to pick them back up again as we leave."

Because of Jesus' sacrifice, all our sins are forgiven without exception. It is that simple and true. We point to His Word and His work for assurance that He has forgiven our sin. Lasting feelings of guilt may mean that we haven't forgiven ourselves, or they could serve to deter us from another sin when we are tempted in the future. But lasting feelings of guilt are not signs that God has failed to keep His Word to forgive those who confess their sins.

When doubts creep in, and they likely will at times, remember the promises God made to you through your Baptism. Next time you go to Communion, listen closely to the words spoken by the pastor of what Jesus willingly endured to ensure your forgiveness. Trust God at His Word. When it comes to the work of forgiveness, Jesus said it best: "It is finished!"

———∽◦C∕⧵◦∽———

CLOSING PRAYER: Saving Lord, thank You for bearing our burdens, forgiving our sins, and giving us Your Spirit and Church to speak Your words of truth to us. Give us faith to trust Your work and lives that reflect it to others. In the name of our Savior, Jesus, we pray. Amen.

The Third Article

... On the Last Day He will raise me and all the dead, and give eternal life to me and all believers in Christ.

—◦◦◦◦◦—

If the Spirit of Him who raised Jesus from the dead dwells in you, He who raised Christ Jesus from the dead will also give life to your mortal bodies through His Spirit who dwells in you. (Romans 8:11)

LUTHER'S WRITINGS ON THE THIRD ARTICLE OF THE APOSTLES' CREED

Now Christ, the Head of Christendom, through whom it lives and has everything, is so great that He fills heaven and earth. Because He has risen from the grave and thereby became a mighty Lord of all things, even of death and hell, as we have heard, we, as His members, must also be affected and touched by His resurrection and must quite certainly participate in what He accomplished with it, since it happened for our sake. As He has taken everything with Him through His resurrection so that both heaven and earth and sun and moon must become new, so He also will bring us with Him, as St. Paul says in 1 Thessalonians 4 [:14] and in Romans 8 [:11] that the same God who has awakened Christ from death will also make our mortal bodies alive, and all creatures, which are now subjected to vanity and anxiously long for our glory, will also be freed from decay and become glorious together with us [Rom. 8:21].

AE 57:134

More Than Halfway — Jonathan Boehne

How's our resurrection coming along? In the sermon quoted here, Luther later states that our resurrection is already halfway there. Even more than half. Jesus is busy at work with us right now. He is risen from the dead and He is working. He is raising us sinners from death to life through His Word and Holy Baptism. We're over halfway.

If you're driving across the country or running a marathon, it's great to be more than halfway there. But we will also groan because we desperately want to be all the way there. It's no different when it comes to our resurrection. We give God all glory and praise that we are already spiritually raised to new life in Jesus. We are baptized and forgiven! At the same time, we also groan deeply for our full and complete resurrection (Romans 8:23). We want to leave this world of sin, death, and decay behind us. And we can barely wait for the glory that will be ours on the Last Day when Jesus will raise our bodies from the dust to perfection and immortality.

Consider a seed planted in the ground. If we had never seen anyone plant a seed in the ground, the entire idea would certainly sound foolish and ignorant. How could a dead seed bring anything good? Yet God uses that seed to produce new life. In the same way, our bodies will truly rise from the dirt, new and glorious. "Behold," He says, "I am making all things new" (Revelation 21:5).

———⋘∘⋙———

CLOSING PRAYER: Father in heaven, You raised Jesus to life and have raised us with Him in Holy Baptism. As we groan for our final resurrection on the Last Day, give us Your Spirit to live faithfully and joyfully in anticipation of the life of the world to come. Through Jesus Christ, our Lord. Amen.

The Close of the Articles

This is most certainly true.

———— ∘◦✺◦∘ ————

So Jesus said to the Jews who had believed Him, "If you abide in My word, you are truly My disciples, and you will know the truth, and the truth will set you free." (John 8:31–32)

Luther's Writings on the Close of the Articles

Therefore we should be prepared in such a manner that even if some of us were to fall away in order to flatter the pope or tyrants and become liars and knaves, everyone may so firmly have laid hold of the Gospel that he is able to stand by himself and to exclaim: Well, I do not believe the Gospel because a certain man has proclaimed and taught it! Let him go and stay where he will! The doctrine is right. This I know, no matter what, in the providence of God, may happen to me and others because of it.

So far I have had to act in this way for myself personally, and I must continue to do so. Otherwise I would have been terrified and tired out when I saw the pope, bishops, the emperor, kings, and all the world opposed to the doctrine which they ought to sustain. Thoughts such as these would have overwhelmed me: See here, after all, they are people too; surely, they cannot all belong to the devil. How can I find comfort and stand firm except by saying: Even if ten more worlds and all that is great, high, wise, and prudent, and all my dear friends and brethren besides desert me, yet the doctrine is right. It stands; nor will it fall as men fall and waver. I will stand by this Word of God no matter what else may stand or fall.

WLS § 4500

Not Fashionable, Just True — Philip Rigdon

The devil does his best lying by mixing falsehood with truth. What's more, he deceives best when wrapping lies in a comforting mantle of benevolence. Satan teaches the value of unity and then preaches that the same is more important than truth. The world lectures on the merits of gentle speech and then condemns the Bible as offensive. Our sinful nature would have us believe that to reject the truth of God's wrath and His grace in Jesus Christ is not merely one option, but the kindest, most enlightened option. *Confess my sins? No, let's think positive! Salvation in Christ alone? C'mon, don't be so narrow!* How many have walked away from Jesus Christ, believing that in doing so they have benefited the world?

Jesus Christ is the divine physician who not only diagnoses the cancer of sin, but also loves me enough to tell me the mortal truth. More important, like no other doctor, Jesus takes your tumor of transgression into Himself. Instead of trying to shrink or excise the sickness, the Savior allows it to kill Him. Through this death, the Son of God nullifies the power of sin and passes this blessing along to sinners. Yes, God tells me I am a sinner, and I believe Him. He also tells me that I am forgiven, and I believe Him. Not because this news is fashionable, enlightened, or even beneficial, but because He is almighty. Forgiveness is a truth not based in cultural shift or political movement, but in the unchanging, eternal God.

CLOSING PRAYER: Dear unchanging Father, protect us from lies that seem progressive, unifying, and beneficial. Thank You for loving us enough to tell the truth of Your righteous justice and tender grace. When all the world, even spouse and child, turn away, direct my heart to the firm reality of salvation in Your Son, Jesus Christ. Amen.

What Is Prayer?

Prayer is speaking to God in words and thoughts.
(SC, Question 231)

———— ◦◦◦◦◦ ————

Rejoice always, pray without ceasing, give thanks
in all circumstances; for this is the will of God in
Christ Jesus for you. (1 Thessalonians 5:16–18)

LUTHER'S WRITINGS ON THE LORD'S PRAYER

But where there is to be a true prayer, there must be seriousness.
People must feel their distress, and such distress presses them and
compels them to call and cry out. Then prayer will be made willingly, as it ought to be. People will need no teaching about how
to prepare for it and to reach the proper devotion. But the distress
that ought to concern us most (both for ourselves and everyone),
you will find abundantly set forth in the Lord's Prayer. Therefore, this prayer also serves as a reminder, so that we meditate
on it and lay it to heart and do not fail to pray. For we all have
enough things that we lack. The great problem is that we do not
feel or recognize this. Therefore, God also requires that you weep
and ask for such needs and wants, not because He does not know
about them [Matthew 6:8], but so that you may kindle your heart
to stronger and greater desires and make wide and open your
cloak to receive much [Psalm 10:17].

LC III 26–27

Our Father Meets Our Needs — James Lamb

He had not been in church for a while. But now he sat in his pastor's office. His first words: "Pastor, it got so bad I had to turn to God." Here we find an example of what Luther meant when he talked about being compelled to "call and cry out." Distress drove this man to his knees with a need he knew he could not meet.

But why wait? Why be driven to our knees when we can fall to our knees? Why let circumstances throw our needs in front of us when we can use the Lord's Prayer? Go through the Lord's Prayer and let it speak of your needs.

Do we honor God's name as holy in everything we do? Are we living joyfully in His kingdom, knowing He rules our lives through His grace? Do we always put His will before our own? What physical needs do we forget to bring before Him? Here's a big one: What do we lack when it comes to forgiving others? Temptations abound. Do we seek God's strength? Evil surrounds. Are we caught up in any of it?

When we meditate on these questions, we find we lack much! But we need not fear. We do not pray to some vengeful God who wants us to shape up or else. We pray to our Father who adopted us through a crucified and risen Jesus. He loves us and forgives us. He gives and wants what's best for us.

———

CLOSING PRAYER: Father, we confess we often wait until things get really bad before we turn to You in prayer. Give us a heart of unceasing prayer, speaking to You in words and thoughts to lay our needs before You. We know You answer for Jesus' sake. Amen.

The Introduction

Our Father who art in heaven.

What does this mean? With these words, God tenderly invites us to believe that He is our true Father and that we are His true children, so that with all boldness and confidence we may ask Him as dear children ask their dear father.

If you then, who are evil, know how to give good gifts to your children, how much more will your Father who is in heaven give good things to those who ask Him! (Matthew 7:11)

LUTHER'S WRITINGS ON THE INTRODUCTION TO THE LORD'S PRAYER

The best way to begin or introduce the prayer is to know how to address, honor, and treat the person to whom we submit our petition, and how to conduct ourselves in his presence, so that he will be gracious toward us and willing to listen to us. Now, of all names there is none that gains us more favor with God than that of "Father." This is indeed a friendly, sweet, intimate, and warm-hearted word. To speak the words "Lord" or "God" or "Judge" would not be nearly as gracious and comforting to us. The name "Father" is part of our nature and is sweet by nature. That is why it is the most pleasing to God, and why no other name moves him so strongly to hear us. With this name we likewise confess that we are the children of God, which again stirs his heart mightily; for there is no lovelier sound than that of a child speaking to his father.

AE 42:22

Approaching the Heavenly Father as a Child — Jonathan Rusnak

My father taught me from an early age, "When someone speaks to you, look that person in the eye and respond. It isn't an option. It's what my children do."

How much greater is the reality that my Creator has spoken to me by His Son (Hebrews 1:2). My soul hears the Spirit-breathed Word and responds to my Father. It's what a child of God does.

As a rebellious creature, I am not worthy to be called a child of God (Luke 15:21). As a lost and condemned person, I cannot approach His presence (Leviticus 21:16–24; Jeremiah 30:21). But the Son has addressed me. More than that, He stands in my place in the Creed so I can stand in His place in this prayer. He prays for me and with me, but He also invites me to pray with Him, to enter with Him into the courts of heaven, to draw near to the throne of grace, and to approach the God of heaven as He does—confidently, with God as my dear Father (John 15:16; Hebrews 4:16). Adopted by the Spirit and addressed by the Son, my Lord and Savior, I respond to the Father.

Jesus is teaching me to approach the Father as He does, boldly and confidently, with dependence and reliance, just like a little child. Jesus goes with me and teaches me to trust His promise to respond. It's what our Father does. He has and He will (Psalm 50:15; Luke 11:13; Romans 8:32).

———— ∘≪◌≫∘ ————

CLOSING PRAYER: Dear Father in heaven, Your Son is faithful to me. Send Your Spirit of adoption that I might join Your Son in prayer, speaking freely and confidently to You without fear of punishment and trusting that You hear me and will respond. Strengthen my faith and move me to pray. In Your name we pray. Amen.

THE LORD'S PRAYER

The First Petition

Hallowed be Thy name.

What does this mean? God's name is certainly holy in itself, but we pray in this petition that it may be kept holy among us also. . . .

⊷◦⟋⟍◦⊶

But God's firm foundation stands, bearing this seal: "The Lord knows those who are His," and, "Let everyone who names the name of the Lord depart from iniquity." (2 Timothy 2:19)

LUTHER'S WRITINGS ON THE FIRST PETITION OF THE LORD'S PRAYER

Thus we Christians, through our rebirth in baptism, became children of God. And if we pattern ourselves after our Father and all his ways, all his goods and names are likewise our inheritance forever. Now, our Father is and is called merciful and good, as Christ says, "Be merciful, even as your Father is merciful" [Luke 6:36]. He also says, "Learn from me; for I am gentle and lowly in heart" [Matt. 11:29]. God is, furthermore, just, pure, truthful, strong, guileless, wise, etc. These are all names of God and are comprehended in the words "thy name," for the names of all virtues are also names given to God. And since we are baptized into these names and are consecrated and hallowed by them, and since they have thus become our names, it follows that God's children should be called and also be gentle, merciful, chaste, just, truthful, guileless, friendly, peaceful, and kindly disposed toward all, even toward our enemies. For the name of God, in which we were baptized, works all this in us. But we should always pray that the name of God may abide in us, be active in us, and be hallowed.

AE 42:28

Baptized into the Name of Grace — Heidi Goehmann

This First Petition of the Lord's Prayer is a good reminder that God doesn't need us, but He does want us. He wants to be a part of our days, our nights, and all our moments. He knows those who are His. He comes to us through His Spirit, given to us in our Baptism, and is active and holy in our families, in our homes, at our dinner table, on the drive to school, through every door we enter and every conversation we have. In this petition, we pray that we would embrace the presence of Jesus Christ, our Savior, in our lives, rather than stuff Him into a neatly confined box to bring out when He is convenient. We pray His mercy would pour out of us into those around us. We pray His gentleness and truth would be found in our words. We pray we would fight for justice in His name in this unjust world. We pray we would be led to open His Word frequently, letting Him give us insight into where the devil would try to fool, kill, and destroy any wisdom for our relationships. Kindness and friendliness are wonderful things, but kindness and friendliness done in *the name of Christ Jesus* are powerful. Undeserved grace given to those we encounter in the name of Jesus mangles and destroys what the devil would try to do in our families, in our relationships, in our churches, and even in our own bodies. All praise be to His name!

CLOSING PRAYER: Lord, we know You are living and active in us, through the Spirit we first received on the day of our Baptism. Today, we pray for ever-increasing awareness of Your abiding and active presence in everything we do and everywhere we go. In Jesus' name we pray. Amen.

The First Petition

How is God's name kept holy? God's name is kept holy when the Word of God is taught in its truth and purity, and we, as the children of God, also lead holy lives according to it. Help us to do this, dear Father in heaven! But anyone who teaches or lives contrary to God's Word profanes the name of God among us. Protect us from this, heavenly Father!

∽○◁∾∾▷○∽

As obedient children, do not be conformed to the passions of your former ignorance, but as He who called you is holy, you also be holy in all your conduct, since it is written, "You shall be holy, for I am holy." (1 Peter 1:14–16)

LUTHER'S WRITINGS ON THE FIRST PETITION OF THE LORD'S PRAYER

Now, God's name is profaned by us either through our words or in our works. (For whatever we do upon the earth must be either words or works, speech or act.) In the first place, then, God's name is profaned when people preach, teach, and say in God's name what is false and misleading. They use His name like an ornament and attract a market for falsehood. That is, indeed, the greatest way to profane and dishonor the divine name. Furthermore, men, by swearing, cursing, conjuring, and other such actions, grossly abuse the holy name as a cloak for their shame [1 Peter 2:16]. In the second place, God's name is profaned by an openly wicked life and works, when those who are called Christians and God's people are adulterers, drunkards, misers, enviers, and slanderers [1 Corinthians 5:11]. Here again God's name must come to shame and be profaned because of us.

LC III 40–43

Hallowed Be Thy Name — David Loy

If you have lived in a small town, then you know how important it is to have a good name—and how difficult it can be if someone in your family has brought shame to your family name. A good reputation opens doors, while a bad reputation closes them. The same can be said for God's name—except that it is us, His sons and daughters, who all too often drag His name through the mud instead of doing the good works that cause others to give glory to our Father in heaven.

We therefore pray that God's name would be hallowed—that is, be treated as holy. His name is special because it is the name of the God—Father, Son, and Holy Spirit—who created, redeemed, and sanctifies us. It is the name of the Lord God who saves us when we call on Him. It is the sign of God's love because with it the almighty Creator of the universe invites us to talk to Him. It would be a sin against His name to drag it through the mud, and it would be a shame to give Him a bad reputation in the world. We pray that His name would be kept holy by other people and most especially by us, who were baptized into His name and who represent it to others. We are saved by His name, so we pray that we treat it as the treasure it is.

———◦◦◦———

CLOSING PRAYER: Our Father in heaven, let everyone treat Your name as the holy treasure it is. When people teach false doctrine in Your name, correct them. When we live contrary to Your Word and bring shame on Your name, move us to repent, and forgive us. In our Lord's name. Amen.

The Second Petition

Thy kingdom come.
What does this mean? The kingdom of God certainly comes by itself without our prayer, but we pray in this petition that it may come to us also. . . .

<hr />

Whoever makes a practice of sinning is of the devil, for the devil has been sinning from the beginning. The reason the Son of God appeared was to destroy the works of the devil. (1 John 3:8)

LUTHER'S WRITINGS ON THE SECOND PETITION OF THE LORD'S PRAYER

Now, all of us dwell in the devil's kingdom until the coming of the kingdom of God. However, there is a difference. To be sure, the godly are also in the devil's kingdom, but they daily and steadfastly contend against sins and resist the lusts of the flesh, the allurements of the world, the whisperings of the devil. After all, no matter how godly we may be, the evil lust always wants to share the reign in us and would like to rule us completely and overcome us. In that way God's kingdom unceasingly engages in combat with the devil's kingdom. And the members of the former are preserved and saved because they, within themselves, fight against the devil's kingdom in order to enlarge the kingdom of God. It is they who pray this petition with words, hearts, and deeds. Thus the holy apostle Paul says that "we must not let sin reign in our mortal bodies, to make us obey its passions" [Rom. 6:12].

AE 42:38–39

Tug-of-War — Heather Culli

Have you ever witnessed a live tug-of-war? The teams straining, the crowds cheering, and the flag in constant flux back and forth across the mid-line all keep spectators engaged and entertained. Evenly matched teams strive to physically outlast each other in a battle of strength. The competition takes an interesting turn, though, when teams are mismatched. The weaker team's strategy is to use logic, rather than brute force, to their advantage. Many a mismatched team has walked to the rope, taken their place, and grabbed hold only to let go once the starter's pistol is fired. It's a brilliant maneuver! When all tension is removed from the rope, the team pulling falls victim to the laws of motion and collapses on the ground. Does the flag cross the line in a seeming victory for the fallen team? Yes. Has the weaker team fallen victim to the strength of the other side? No. Quite the opposite.

Luther uses the phrase "engage in combat" to describe the war taking place between the kingdom of the devil and the kingdom of God. No amount of human striving can keep sinners from the temptations that so easily entangle our hearts and minds. It is Jesus alone who saves. Just as a team pulling on the rope has no power over those who have let go, so the devil has no power over those redeemed by Christ. Through Jesus' death and resurrection, the tension in the struggle for our souls is released. Satan may think he has triumphed as he looks out over a sinful world. But in the world that is to come, he already stands defeated. The kingdom of God reigns victorious!

~∘⌒∘~

CLOSING PRAYER: Dear heavenly Father, thank You for sending Your Son to destroy the works of the devil. Preserve and save us as we fight against Satan in his earthly kingdom so that we may rejoice with You and Your Son in Your heavenly kingdom, now and forevermore. Amen.

The Second Petition

How does God's kingdom come? God's kingdom comes
when our heavenly Father gives us His Holy Spirit, so that
by His grace we believe His holy Word and lead godly
lives here in time and there in eternity.

———————◦○◦◦◦———————

According to His great mercy, He has caused us to be born
again to a living hope through the resurrection of Jesus
Christ from the dead, to an inheritance that is imperishable, undefiled, and unfading, kept in heaven for you, who
by God's power are being guarded through faith for a salvation ready to be revealed in the last time. (1 Peter 1:3–5)

LUTHER'S WRITINGS ON THE SECOND PETITION OF THE LORD'S PRAYER

For the coming of God's kingdom to us happens in two ways: (a)
here in time through the Word and faith [Matthew 13]; and (b) in
eternity forever through revelation [Luke 19:11; 1 Peter 1:4–5].
Now we pray for both these things. We pray that the kingdom
may come to those who are not yet in it, and, by daily growth that
it may come to us who have received it, both now and hereafter in
eternal life. All this is nothing other than saying, "Dear Father, we
pray, give us first Your Word, so that the Gospel may be preached
properly throughout the world. Second, may the Gospel be
received in faith and work and live in us, so that through the
Word and the Holy Spirit's power [Romans 15:18–19], Your
kingdom may triumph among us. And we pray that the devil's
kingdom be put down [Luke 11:17–20], so that he may have no
right or power over us [Luke 10:17–19; Colossians 1], until at last
his power may be utterly destroyed. So sin, death, and hell shall

be exterminated [Revelation 20:13–14]. Then we may live forever in perfect righteousness and blessedness" [Ephesians 4:12–13].

LC III 53–54

Ruling and Reigning — Scott Rauch

God rules and reigns the way He wishes. What God says, His truth, goes no matter what. Life with God is about following the King as He understands following. When Jesus says He is "the way, and the truth, and the life" (John 14:6), He is expressing what it means for Him to lead, to be the King. God the Father brings His kingdom through Jesus Christ by the Holy Spirit's power into our world. He invites us in faith to confess this and live well with Him as King. And what a King He is!

His Word is not just something to be written down as cool thoughts to be remembered when we have a moment. His Word, who is Jesus, brings us everything we need for daily life. Our King actively takes the battle to our sinfulness, to the power of Satan, and to death. All have been defeated through Jesus' death and resurrection. The very life of King Jesus, who lives in those who have been baptized and believe, now leads us in our daily living. His rule is one of love and power lived out as He sees fit—which means through His Church, His very people.

His reign does not have term limits. There is no successor-in-waiting. Our King has always been and will always be. We rejoice as we faithfully follow our King in life. Long live "us" because our King reigns!

———⟡———

CLOSING PRAYER: O King of the universe, deliver us from our enemies. Bless us with Your presence. Call us into service with You. We hallow Your name and praise You as King, for Jesus' sake. Amen.

The Third Petition

Thy will be done on earth as it is in heaven.

What does this mean? The good and gracious will of God is done even without our prayer, but we pray in this petition that it may be done among us also. . . .

<hr>

And He withdrew from them about a stone's throw, and knelt down and prayed, saying, "Father, if You are willing, remove this cup from me. Nevertheless, not My will, but Yours, be done." (Luke 22:41–42)

LUTHER'S WRITINGS ON THE THIRD PETITION OF THE LORD'S PRAYER

In this petition you will notice that God bids us to pray against ourselves. In that way he teaches us that we have no greater enemy than ourself. You see, our will is the most formidable element in us, and against it we must pray, "O Father, do not let me get to the point where my will is done. Break my will; resist it. No matter what happens let my life be governed not by my will, but by yours. As no one's own will prevails in heaven so may it also be here on earth." Such a petition or its fulfillment is indeed very painful to our human nature, for our own will is the greatest and most deep-rooted evil in us, and nothing is dearer to us than our own will.

Therefore, we are asking for nothing else in this petition than the cross, torment, adversity, and sufferings of every kind, since these serve the destruction of our will. If these self-willed people really thought about this and noted that they are praying against their own will, they would turn against this petition or even be frightened by it.

AE 42:48–49

Battle of the Wills — Faith Spelbring

A three-year-old girl sat at the dinner table. Her uneaten food was the only thing left on the table. It had been forty-five minutes since the rest of her family had cleared their plates and enjoyed dessert. No amount of bribery or threats would get the girl to eat. Even though she usually liked the dish, this particular night she simply refused to eat it and demanded something else.

When in faith we pray, "Thy will be done," we are asking God to ignore the three-year-old who lives inside us and screams, "*My* will be done!" To utter these words is admitting to God that His ways are better than ours. Even when we don't understand His ways, they are better than ours.

To utter the words "Thy will be done!" in prayer to our Lord requires one of two things: either total laziness to rattle off words without thinking about what we are saying, or great and God-given faith to bravely ask God to ignore our selfish will and enact His good and gracious will, even if we do not comprehend or like it.

When one considers the selfish nature of humans in comparison to the good and gracious character of our God, revealed especially in Jesus, our Savior, perhaps it is wise to pray these words after all.

CLOSING PRAYER: "Take my will and make it Thine, It shall be no longer mine; Take my heart, it is Thine own, It shall be Thy royal throne" (*LSB* 783:5). Amen.

The Third Petition

How is God's will done? God's will is done when He breaks
and hinders every evil plan and purpose of the devil, the world,
and our sinful nature, which do not want us to hallow God's
name or let His kingdom come; and when He strengthens and
keeps us firm in His Word and faith until we die. This is His
good and gracious will.

———◦◦◦———

And this is the will of Him who sent Me, that I
should lose nothing of all that He has given Me,
but raise it up on the last day. (John 6:39)

LUTHER'S WRITINGS ON THE THIRD PETITION OF THE LORD'S PRAYER

"If you perceive My will," He wants to say, "you also perceive
the Father's will and goodness, and you need not fear the Father."
Your heart should not say: "Yes, Lord Jesus, I believe Thy words
assuring me that Thou wilt not cast me out; but what if the Father
were ungracious toward me and wanted to reject me?" "No,"
He replies, "there is no longer any wrath in heaven if you are at
peace with Me. For the Father brought you to Me. He shares My
will. He taught you to know Me and to believe in Me. His will
and Mine are identical. If He had resolved to destroy and reject
you, He would not have brought you to Me and left you with
Me. Nor would He have given you His Word, faith, Baptism, and
the knowledge and the acceptance of this sublime article of faith.
Therefore you must not make a distinction between My will and
that of My Father; for it is My will not to cast you out, and that
is also My Father's will. I will not condemn you; nor will He."

AE 23:61–62

Don't Make It Complicated — Jonathan Boehne

Math can be extremely challenging to even the brightest students. Yet all of math is simply counting. Addition, multiplication, fractions, algebra, and geometry are all advanced counting. God's will can likewise be challenging for Christians to discern in certain arenas of life. And yet all of God's will is simply faith in Jesus. God's will for us is that we believe.

Is it God's will for us to do other good works as well? Yes, certainly it is. But first and foremost, His will is always that we believe in Jesus and never be cast out. So He gives us His Word. And He keeps us firm in that Word until we die. And then He will raise us up to see Jesus face-to-face. That's His will.

Truthfully, God's will isn't the most challenging will for Christians. Rather, it's the other wills that are lined up for battle against God's will. The devil's will is that we don't believe in Jesus or His Word. The world's will is to take all power and glory for ourselves rather than trust in the power and glory of God. And even our own flesh wants to be god rather than believe in God. So we pray for God to break their wills.

If we believe in Jesus, we are doing the will of God. After that, we can talk about His other will for us to love Him and love one another. But only after some simple counting—God counting our faith in Christ as righteousness (Romans 4:5).

CLOSING PRAYER: Father, You have not counted our trespasses against us but, through faith in Christ, have counted us righteous. Break and hinder every will of the devil, the world, and our flesh that would keep us from faith. Give us Your Spirit to believe in Jesus. Through Jesus Christ, our Lord. Amen.

The Fourth Petition

Give us this day our daily bread.

What does this mean? God certainly gives daily bread to everyone without our prayers, even to all evil people, but we pray in this petition that God would lead us to realize this and to receive our daily bread with thanksgiving. . . .

―――――∞⟨◇⟩∞―――――

Every good gift and every perfect gift is from above, coming down from the Father of lights with whom there is no variation or shadow due to change. (James 1:17)

LUTHER'S WRITINGS ON THE FOURTH PETITION OF THE LORD'S PRAYER

You see, in this way, God wishes to show us how He cares for us in all our need and faithfully provides also for our earthly support. He abundantly grants and preserves these things, even for the wicked and rogues [Matthew 5:45]. Yet, He wishes that we pray for these goods in order that we may recognize that we receive them from His hand and may feel His fatherly goodness toward us in them [Psalm 104:28; 145:16]. For when He withdraws His hand, nothing can prosper or be maintained in the end. Indeed, we daily see this and experience it. How much trouble there is now in the world only on account of bad coins, daily oppression, raising of prices in common trade, and bargaining and labor by those who greedily oppress the poor and deprive them of their daily bread! This we must suffer indeed. But let such people take care so that they do not lose the benefits of common intercession. Let them beware lest this petition in the Lord's Prayer speak against them.

LC III 82–84

That We Would Know His Fatherly Goodness — Philip Rigdon

James includes an interesting phrase: "coming down from the Father" (1:17). Christians and unbelievers alike wonder why God doesn't provide according to their expectations. "A loving God would give everyone a million dollars!" "Lord, I need a job today; what are You waiting for?" Recall Exodus 16, when God sent manna to the Israelites in the desert. The Lord instructed the people to take what they needed for each day. Their heavenly Father would certainly provide, but in such a manner that the people would be mindful of Him. Were God to give all we wanted or even needed immediately, we would be apt to disregard Him and waste all that He has provided. Remember the prodigal son?

We should never doubt or be surprised that God desires to and will provide our earthly needs. Why would He be stingy with food, clothing, or home when He has given us His very self in the Son, our Savior, Jesus Christ? God provides for all people, Christians and unbelievers alike, blessing those who are His children and reaching out to those who are not. Beyond all the earthly needs and wants God satisfies, He knows that the most precious gift is life eternal with Him. Jesus took on Himself the burden of our sins in order to bring sinners back to Himself. Our heavenly Father longs to bring home His prodigal sons and daughters. For when we have Him, all the provisions of this world will seem vain and pale.

CLOSING PRAYER: Dear heavenly Father, we are as faithful in our complaints and doubts as You are in goodness and mercy. As You care for our needs, lead us to care for others. Keep us ever mindful that You are the good and perfect gift from above, the manna that is new every morning. In Your name we pray. Amen.

The Fourth Petition

What is meant by daily bread? Daily bread includes everything that has to do with the support and needs of the body, such as food, drink, clothing, shoes, house, home, land, animals, money, goods, a devout husband or wife, devout children, devout workers, devout and faithful rulers, good government, good weather, peace, health, self-control, good reputation, good friends, faithful neighbors, and the like.

⸺◦◦⸺

Man shall not live by bread alone, but by every word that comes from the mouth of God. (Matthew 4:4)

LUTHER'S WRITINGS ON THE FOURTH PETITION OF THE LORD'S PRAYER

This petition means to say, "O heavenly Father, since no one likes your will and since we are too weak to have our will and our old Adam mortified, we pray that you will feed us, strengthen and comfort us with your holy Word, and grant us your grace that the heavenly bread, Jesus Christ, may be preached and heard in all the world, that we may know it in our hearts, and so that all harmful, heretical, erroneous, and human doctrine may cease and only your Word, which is truly our living bread, be distributed. But do we not also pray for our physical bread? Answer: Yes, this too may well be included in this petition. However, this petition refers principally to Christ, the spiritual bread of the soul. This is why Christ teaches us not to worry about our body's food and raiment, but to take thought only for the needs of each day.

AE 42:61–62

Give Us This Day ... Jesus! — James Lamb

Round one to Jesus! As He would in rounds two and three of those wilderness temptations, Jesus pins His wicked and wily foe to the mat. He does so with the Word of God. Jesus does not belittle the need for physical bread. After forty days without food, He knew that need very well! But bread "alone" will not suffice. We also need "every word" that comes from God.

Luther does not belittle the need for physical bread when it comes to his explanation of the Fourth Petition. Indeed, his list of what that includes challenges our memorization skills! In this petition, we pray for these things and we acknowledge their source, our heavenly Father.

But the Fourth Petition also reminds us of our Father's greatest blessing, the bread of life. Jesus is "the living bread that came down from heaven" (John 6:51). He came down pure and unspoiled. Then He "went bad." God placed the sin that spoils us on Him. Jesus suffered the wrath of God so we never have to. Through faith in this resurrected and living bread, we have new life. We have forgiveness. We live covered by His purity.

Continue to pray for daily bread and thankfully enjoy God's blessings. But also pray, "Give us this day Jesus." We need this bread to strengthen our faith, to turn our will to His, and to give us hope in the midst of life's many struggles.

CLOSING PRAYER: Heavenly Father, we thank You for our daily bread. Forgive us when we are unthankful and take for granted Your gracious provision. Keep us mindful of those who might be in need and use us to provide for them. But above all else, we pray that You give us this day Jesus. Amen.

The Fifth Petition

And forgive us our trespasses as we forgive those who trespass against us.

What does this mean? We pray in this petition that our Father in heaven would not look at our sins, or deny our prayer because of them. We are neither worthy of the things for which we pray, nor have we deserved them, but we ask that He would give them all to us by grace, for we daily sin much and surely deserve nothing but punishment. So we too will sincerely forgive and gladly do good to those who sin against us.

———— ∞◦∽◦∞ ————

I acknowledged my sin to You, and I did not cover my iniquity; I said, "I will confess my transgressions to the LORD," and You forgave the iniquity of my sin. Therefore let everyone who is godly offer prayer to You at a time when You may be found. (Psalm 32:5–6)

LUTHER'S WRITINGS ON THE FIFTH PETITION OF THE LORD'S PRAYER

But this should serve God's purpose of breaking our pride and keeping us humble. God has reserved this right for Himself: if anyone wants to boast of his godliness and despise others, that person is to think about himself and place this prayer before his eyes. . . . Let no one think as long as he lives here he can reach such a position that he will not need such forgiveness [1 John 1:8]. In short, if God does not forgive without stopping, we are lost. It is, therefore, the intent of this petition that God would not regard our sins and hold up to us what we daily deserve. But we pray that He would deal graciously with us and forgive, as He has promised, and so grant us a joyful and confident conscience to stand before Him in prayer [Hebrews 10:22]. For where the heart is not in a right relationship with God, or cannot take such confidence, it will not dare to pray anymore. Such a confident and joyful heart can spring from nothing else than the certain knowledge of the forgiveness of sin [Psalm 32:1–2; Romans 4:7–8].

LC III 90–92

Forgiveness That Freely Flows — Jonathan Rusnak

We lived in the basement with six apartments above us. I am not a plumber. So, when the sewer backed up, I made a phone call. Tree roots had plugged up the pipes. My own sewage is bad enough, but the fountain that flowed from my shower drain was much more.

Our God is an eternal fountain (Psalm 68:26). He delivers pure, life-giving water (Zechariah 13:1; John 4:13–14). Through His Son and in His Spirit, His grace flows freely (John 19:34; Hebrews 10:22; 1 John 1:7). Should that spring cease, so do we (Psalm 36:9). But the river of life that flows from Him will never run dry (Revelation 22:1).

Saturated in our own sewage, we come to Him for cleansing. He goes to work through water, Word, bread, and wine. He removes the guilt of our own sin and the shame of being stained by everyone else's. Once we are again cleansed, He unstops our lips and fills our mouths with prayer and praise (Psalm 51:15).

If His fountain flows so freely to us, why do we stop it up so easily (Proverbs 25:26)? We let others' sin simmer like sewage in our souls. It's a toxic, deadly mess. Like cracked containers, we fail to deliver the forgiveness God pours out so freely to us (Jeremiah 2:13; Matthew 18:21–35).

But the forgiveness is His. He is the fountain, the water, and the master plumber. As His forgiveness flows freely to us, He works that it might flow freely through us.

⸎

CLOSING PRAYER: Dear heavenly Father, You forgive freely through Your Son, Jesus Christ, and by Your Holy Spirit. Forgive again my unbelief and stopped-up soul. Work in me that I might freely forgive as I have been freely forgiven. In Your name we pray. Amen.

The Sixth Petition

And lead us not into temptation.

What does this mean? God tempts no one. We pray in this petition that God would guard and keep us so that the devil, the world, and our sinful nature may not deceive us or mislead us into false belief, despair, and other great shame and vice. Although we are attacked by these things, we pray that we may finally overcome them and win the victory.

No temptation has overtaken you that is not common to man. God is faithful, and He will not let you be tempted beyond your ability, but with the temptation He will also provide the way of escape, that you may be able to endure it. (1 Corinthians 10:13)

LUTHER'S WRITINGS ON THE SIXTH PETITION OF THE LORD'S PRAYER

We are frequently tempted by thoughts of despair; for what human being is there who could be without this thought: "What if God did not want you to be saved?" But we are taught that in this conflict we must hold fast to the promise given us in Baptism, which is sure and clear. But when this happens, Satan does not cease immediately but keeps crying out in your heart that you are not worthy of this promise.

But in this situation there is need of the fervent prayer that God may give us His Spirit, in order that the promise may not be wrested from us. I am unable to resolve this contradiction. Our only consolation is that in affliction we take refuge in the promise; for it alone is our staff and rod, and if Satan strikes it out of our hands, we have no place left to stand. But we must hold fast to the promise and maintain that, just as the text states about Abraham, we are tempted by God, not because He really wants this, but because He wants to find out whether we love Him above all things and are able to bear Him when He is angry as we gladly bear Him when He is beneficent and makes promises.

AE 4:93

The Sword against Temptation: The Word — Heidi Goehmann

God wants actual relationship with us, not a false relationship, not half a relationship, and not a pretend version of relationship. Because God values relationship with us so highly, He presents His actual self to us in His Word, rather than a version of Him that may be more comfortable and more palatable to handle. Temptation, God's anger, how they interact, and our sinner/saint reality can be confusing and can lead us to despair. Satan likes to kick us while we're down and put lies in our ears about who we are and who God is. Satan whispers, "God doesn't want you. God doesn't want to hear your sin. You should despair, fall into shame."

The Word in our lives saves us from despair, shame, and vice. The Word tells us who God is and all that He has done for us. We cling to God's Word not to avoid temptation, but to walk through temptation with Christ before us and beside us, the sword of the Spirit valiantly swinging, the helmet of salvation firm on our heads, our feet shod with God's peace even when we have a hard time finding exact answers to our questions.

Temptation is common. It will come to us. But our triune God is anything but common, and we trust that His promises are better, brighter, and stronger than anything Satan can toss our way. To Him be glory forever. He saves us!

------◦◦◦◦◦------

CLOSING PRAYER: Lord, You know the temptations that are common to man and common to me. Sometimes I make a mess of life, but You have promised never to leave me or forsake me. Be with me on this daily walk, as You have promised. In Jesus' name I ask it. Amen.

The Seventh Petition

But deliver us from evil.

What does this mean? We pray in this petition, in summary, that our Father in heaven would rescue us from every evil of body and soul, possessions and reputation, and finally, when our last hour comes, give us a blessed end, and graciously take us from this valley of sorrow to Himself in heaven.

⋘━━━━━━━⋙

We know that we are from God, and the whole world lies in the power of the evil one. (1 John 5:19)

LUTHER'S WRITINGS ON THE SEVENTH PETITION OF THE LORD'S PRAYER

Therefore, we finally sum it all up and say, "Dear Father, grant that we be rid of all these disasters." But there is also included in this petition whatever evil may happen to us under the devil's kingdom: poverty, shame, death, and, in short, all the agonizing misery and heartache of which there is such an unnumbered multitude on the earth. Since the devil is not only a liar, but also a murderer [John 8:44], he constantly seeks our life. He wreaks his vengeance whenever he can afflict our bodies with misfortune and harm. Therefore, it happens that he often breaks men's necks or drives them to insanity, drowns some, and moves many to commit suicide and to many other terrible disasters [e.g., Mark 9:17–22]. So there is nothing for us to do upon earth but to pray against this archenemy without stopping. For unless God preserved us, we would not be safe from this enemy even for an hour.

LC III 114–16

Overcoming Suffering — David Loy

When God created the world, it was very good. And it was for us. He made plants for us to eat, animals to accompany us, and the sun and moon to mark time and give us light. He instituted marriage so we could delight in our spouse and in the children who spring from our love. And in the beginning, we had Him. He walked in the garden with Adam and Eve, and He talked to them face-to-face. It was all very good.

But Satan, who had already rebelled against God, could not abide God's good creation. Knowing God's command to Adam and Eve, he entered the garden and tempted them to eat what was forbidden. They did, and they brought on themselves the curse: division from each other, separation from God, death. And death still stalks us, wreaking havoc through natural disasters, human pride, violence, disease, and the like. We are mostly safe—until we are not. We suffer, and Satan rejoices.

God, however, suffered with us in the person of His Son, Jesus Christ. He died under our curse and rose again victorious. In Him, we also have the victory over death and Satan. We therefore pray to God that He would protect us from all the evils that Satan so gladly sees us suffer. And we know that, whatever evils we experience in this life, we will overcome them all in Christ and once again see God face-to-face on the Last Day.

CLOSING PRAYER: Merciful Father, look with kindness on us sinful creatures, and protect us from the assaults of the evil one. We certainly do not deserve Your protection, but for the sake of Jesus, hear us, preserve us, and bring us to everlasting bliss with You. Through Jesus Christ, our Lord. Amen.

The Conclusion

For Thine is the kingdom and the power and the glory forever and ever. Amen.

What does this mean? This means that I should be certain that these petitions are pleasing to our Father in heaven, and are heard by Him; for He Himself has commanded us to pray in this way and has promised to hear us. Amen, amen means "yes, yes, it shall be so."

⟡

For all the promises of God find their Yes in Him. That is why it is through Him that we utter our Amen to God for His glory. (2 Corinthians 1:20)

LUTHER'S WRITINGS ON THE CONCLUSION OF THE LORD'S PRAYER

Finally, mark this, that you must always speak the Amen firmly. Never doubt that God in his mercy will surely hear you and say "yes" to your prayers. Never think that you are kneeling or standing alone, rather think that the whole of Christendom, all devout Christians, are standing there beside you and you are standing among them in a common, united petition which God cannot disdain. Do not leave your prayer without having said or thought, "Very well, God has heard my prayer; this I know as a certainty and a truth." That is what Amen means.

AE 43:198

The End — Heather Culli

Take a moment and make a list of ten circumstances that signal an ending. What did your list include? Maybe you thought of checking the last box on a to-do list or a curtain falling after the closing act of a performance, or perhaps you flashed back to the sound of the final bell on the last day of school. Take a moment and notice something about your list. Very often, the end of an event mirrors the beginning. Fireworks shows are one of my favorite examples. A loud, colorful bang signals the beginning. The tempo and intensity build until the grand finale culminates in a glorious burst of sound and color. When done right, the ending leaves you shaken and awestruck.

Reading the Lord's Prayer also brings us full circle while providing a thrilling conclusion. The prayer begins with our eyes turned heavenward toward our Father. The focus then turns earthward as we acknowledge our desire to live in a world where God's name is revered and His perfect will is done. Realizing that our sin separates us from this reality, we humble ourselves before God, asking Him to provide first for our earthly needs, then for our spiritual needs as well. Our eyes once again turn heavenward as our requests turn to praise, declaring with renewed vigor the might and majesty of our heavenly Father. The amen caps it all off with a proclamation in the certainty of God's attention and intervention. It's truly a moment that leaves you shaken and awestruck.

———⊶⦚⦉⦚⊷———

CLOSING PRAYER: Dear heavenly Father, You are the Alpha and Omega, the beginning and the end. Thank You for sending Your Son, Jesus, to be our example in prayer. Please forgive us when we fail to approach You humbly, praise You boldly, or rely on You only. To You be the power and glory, now and forever. Amen.

The Means of Grace

Why does the catechism include Baptism, Confession and the Office of the Keys, and the Sacrament of the Altar?
A. The Gospel is given to us in God's written or spoken Word, especially in the Absolution.
B. The Gospel Word is also joined to earthly elements in sacred acts that Christ has given—namely, Baptism and the Lord's Supper. (SC, Question 292)

———∞⟨∞⟩∞———

So faith comes from hearing, and hearing
through the word of Christ. (Romans 10:17)

LUTHER'S WRITINGS ON THE MEANS OF GRACE

Now when God sends forth his holy gospel he deals with us in a twofold manner, first outwardly, then inwardly. Outwardly he deals with us through the oral word of the gospel and through the material signs, that is, baptism and the sacrament of the altar. Inwardly he deals with us through the Holy Spirit, faith, and other gifts. But whatever their measure or order the outward factors should and must precede. The inward experience follows and is effected by the outward. God has determined to give the inward to no one except through the outward. For he wants to give no one the Spirit or faith outside of the outward Word and sign instituted by him, as he says in Luke 16[:29], "Let them hear Moses and the prophets." Accordingly Paul can call baptism a "washing of regeneration" wherein God "richly pours out the Holy Spirit" [Titus 3:5]. And the oral gospel "is the power of God for salvation to every one who has faith" (Rom. 1[:16]).

AE 40:146

The Workshop of God — Scott Rauch

Blueprints. Lists. Tools. Materials. Workbench. Patience. Determination. Care. Discipline. Joy. All of these put together by a master craftsman produce a work that is meant to be both artistic and functional for daily living. The master craftsman "sees" what he will create and then creates what will be seen in the world.

God, our master craftsman, working through His Means of Grace, brings to us the materials and tools by which our very lives are saved for His best works. With written and spoken Scripture, with water, and with bread and wine, we are worked on faithfully by the Holy Spirit to bring the love and grace of Jesus into and out of each of our lives. We are made into new, beautiful creations through which the very life of Jesus functionally works in the world. We are crafted in ways only God can do to be the works of God in our homes and communities.

We are invited to be miniature craftspeople. We are to use the very Word made flesh who lives in us to share God's love and grace in the artistic, functional ways that God has created for us in our lives. For the joy set before Jesus, He saved us. For the joy set before us, we live Him out. Let's get to work!

<hr/>

CLOSING PRAYER: Father, through faith, You have crafted the grace and love of Jesus in our lives. Through the Holy Spirit, work in us the life of Jesus that we might joyfully share in Your work. In Jesus' name. Amen.

The Sacraments

What is a sacrament?

The Lutheran Church usually speaks of a sacrament as a sacred act

A. instituted by the command of Christ;

B. in which Christ joins His Word of promise to a visible element;

C. by which He offers and bestows the forgiveness of sins He has earned for us by His suffering, death, and resurrection. (SC, Question 293)

> For no one is a Jew who is merely one outwardly, nor is circumcision outward and physical. But a Jew is one inwardly, and circumcision is a matter of the heart, by the Spirit, not by the letter. His praise is not from man but from God. (Romans 2:28–29)

LUTHER'S WRITINGS ON THE SACRAMENTS

The same God who now saves us by baptism and the bread, saved Abel by his sacrifice, Noah by the rainbow, Abraham by circumcision, and all the others by their respective signs. So far as the signs are concerned, there is no difference between a sacrament of the Old Law and one of the New. . . . But our signs or sacraments, as well as those of the fathers, have attached to them a word of promise which requires faith, and they cannot be fulfilled by any other work. Hence they are signs or sacraments of justification, for they are sacraments of justifying faith and not of works. Their whole efficacy, therefore, consists in faith itself, not in the doing of a work. Whoever believes them, fulfills them, even if he should not do a single work. This is the origin of the saying: "Not the sacrament, but the faith of the sacrament, justifies." Thus circumcision did not justify Abraham and his seed, and yet the Apostle calls it the seal of the righteousness by faith [Rom.

4:11], because faith in the promise, to which circumcision was added, justified him and fulfilled what the circumcision signified.

AE 36:65–66

A Gift and a Promise — Faith Spelbring

In the Broadway musical *Annie*, Daddy Warbucks came to love the orphan Annie as if she were his own daughter. He planned to give her the gift of a new locket to replace her old and broken one, then reveal his desire to adopt her. When she opened the gift, however, Annie quickly explained that her broken locket was more than it appeared to be. It was a gift from her parents, given to her with a promise attached to it: that they would come back for her one day. Apart from the promise, Annie's locket would have been an ordinary necklace. But because it was attached to a promise, it was of great value to her and simply irreplaceable.

Our God has given us His Word attached to things that may look ordinary—water, bread, wine—but through them, He delivers to us the forgiveness of sins, life, and salvation. Unlike Annie's parents, who left her at an orphanage and could not deliver on their promise to return, our God never leaves us and always keeps His promises.

Through the Word and the waters of Baptism, God delivers on His promise to wash us clean from sin by connecting us to Jesus' death and resurrection. Through the Word in, with, and under bread and wine, God delivers on His promise to forgive our sin by connecting us to the body and blood of Jesus. There is no better gift we could receive than eternal life and salvation from our loving Father!

CLOSING PRAYER: Father, You commanded Baptism and instituted the Lord's Supper for us. Through these sacraments, You forgive our sins and give us life and salvation. Though we do not deserve such grace, we thank You that it is ours because of Your Son, our Savior, in whose name we pray. Amen.

Holy Baptism, Part 1

What is Baptism?

Baptism is not just plain water, but it is the water included in God's command and combined with God's word. . . .

———⚬◦⚬———

There is one body and one Spirit—just as you were called to the one hope that belongs to your call—one Lord, one faith, one baptism, one God and Father of all, who is over all and through all and in all. (Ephesians 4:4–6)

LUTHER'S WRITINGS ON HOLY BAPTISM

Who, then, would despise the fact that God the Father, Son, and Holy Spirit are present? Who would call such water simple water only? Do we not see what sort of spice God casts into this water? If you cast sugar into water, it is no longer water but delicious claret or something else. Why, then, do we want to separate the Word from the water so entirely in this case and say that the water is simple water only, just as if God's Word, nay, God Himself, were not present with and in this water? Not so; for God the Father, Son, and Holy Spirit are indeed in and with this water, as they were there on the banks of the Jordan when Christ stood in the water, the Holy Spirit hovered over it, and God the Father spoke. This is why Baptism is a water that takes away sin, death, and every evil and helps us to enter heaven and eternal life. Such a delicious sugar water, aromatic, and specific it has become because God Himself has entered it.

WLS § 134

Sweet Water — Jonathan Boehne

Luther talks of casting sugar into water to make delicious drinks. Many dollars are spent today on our sugary sodas, juices, coffees, and teas. If you take away the sugar and call them diet, they're just not the same. When it comes to Baptism, the minute you take away the Word of God, you make it nothing. If we don't have the Word of God with that water in the baptismal font, then all we have is a silly and meaningless ritual.

God's Word makes the water of Baptism sweet. When the Israelites tried the desert water at Marah, it was bitter. But God's Word made it sweet when He told Moses to toss in a piece of wood (Exodus 15:25). During the time of Elisha, the men of Jericho came to him because their water was bad and causing sickness and death. At God's word, Elisha took a bowl of salt and threw it in the water. The water was healed (2 Kings 2:22).

How sweet the water of Baptism becomes when the Word of God is added! Sweeter than honey and sugar (Psalm 119:103)! This "Word-water" of Baptism becomes living water that has the power to drive away our bitter sin and death and open the doors of sweet paradise. Even more than that, God Himself comes to us in that "Word-water" and makes His home with us through the work of the Holy Spirit. Be assured that there is nothing silly or meaningless whenever God's Word is present.

———⟶∘⟸⟶∘⟵———

CLOSING PRAYER: Lord, the waters of Baptism are sweet with Your life-giving Word to wash away our sin and give us new life. Keep all sin and bitterness from us and lead us to Your sweet Word of forgiveness. Through Jesus Christ, our Lord. Amen.

Holy Baptism

Which is that word of God?

Christ our Lord says in the last chapter of Matthew: "Therefore go and make disciples of all nations, baptizing them in the name of the Father and of the Son and of the Holy Spirit." (Matt. 28:19)

―――――∘◦⟨≫⟩◦∘―――――

If you love Me, you will keep My commandments. (John 14:15)

LUTHER'S WRITINGS ON HOLY BAPTISM

Just listen to His words: "Go and baptize all nations in the name of the Father and of the Son and of the Holy Spirit" [Matt. 28:19]. "Whoever believes and is baptized is saved," etc. [Mark 16:16]. These are not the words which we speak over the Baptism, but the words of command which institute Baptism. For it is not the priest or minister but He who makes Baptism who says, "Go and baptize," that is, "Here you have My command and order. This is My will and bidding: that you baptize in the name of the Father, Son, and Holy Spirit. If anyone receives the Word and water together, it is a Baptism; if anyone believes in addition, he will be saved thereby." Here there is something beyond the two parts of Word and water; otherwise it would be far from sufficient to dip in water and speak the words "I baptize you," etc.—even if faith were present—without having a clear, certain command to do so.

AE 57:150

Holy Baptism Gives and Takes Away — Philip Rigdon

Restaurants with public restrooms feature signs indicating "EMPLOY-EES MUST WASH HANDS BEFORE RETURNING TO WORK." Such a sign has dual purposes: to remind staff to wash and to assure patrons that this business takes cleanliness seriously. Those who disregard this injunction endanger not only themselves but also everyone and everything they touch. Sadly, many Christians display the same indifference concerning Holy Baptism. Holy Baptism is so vital that our Lord commands it. Holy Baptism is concerned not with preventing the common cold or warding off food-borne illness, but rather with salvation, eternity, heaven, and hell. Yet, like the callow youth who is too busy to wash before returning to work, we care little for Jesus' injunction to take this saving Sacrament to the world.

Hand soaps found in many bathrooms include both a germ-killing agent and a moisturizer. Such a soap takes away but also adds. So it is with Holy Baptism. Holy Baptism removes our sins, past, present, and future. God doesn't stop there. In this Sacrament, God creates saving faith, grants eternal life, and gives us His Holy Spirit. He makes us His child forever. Our own Baptism connects us to Jesus' Baptism in the Jordan River, to His sinless life and innocent suffering. In other words, God sees His Son when He looks at one who has been baptized. God commands His Church to baptize, not that man's efforts would save, but rather that sinners would be saved through Jesus' efforts.

CLOSING PRAYER: Dear Lord, in our selfishness, we would have the benefits of Your Baptism and yet neglect to bring these gifts to others. Change our hearts that we would love others as You do. Make us ever mindful that this gift of Holy Baptism brings to us the fruits of Your loving labor in Christ. In Your name we pray. Amen.

Holy Baptism, Part 2

What benefits does Baptism give?

It works the forgiveness of sins, rescues from death and the devil, and gives eternal salvation to all who believe this, as the words and promises of God declare. . . .

⟿

Baptism, which corresponds to this, now saves you.
(1 Peter 3:21)

LUTHER'S WRITINGS ON HOLY BAPTISM

To correct this wickedness God has devised the plan of making our flesh altogether new, even as Jeremiah [18:4–6] shows. For the potter, when the vessel "was spoiled in his hand," thrust it again into the lump of clay and kneaded it, and afterward made another vessel, as seemed good to him. "So," says God, "are you in my hands." In the first birth we are spoiled; therefore he thrusts us into the earth again by death, and makes us over at the Last Day, that we may be perfect and without sin.

This plan, as has been said, begins in baptism, which signifies death and the resurrection at the Last Day. Therefore so far as the sign of the sacrament and its significance are concerned, sins and the man are both already dead, and he has risen again; and so the sacrament has taken place. But the work of the sacrament has not yet been fully done, which is to say that death and the resurrection at the Last Day are still before us.

AE 35:32

Living Underwater — James Lamb

Living underwater in the womb is wonderful! We live and move in the watery world of the amniotic fluid. The cushiony walls of the womb protect us. We swim, tread water, kick, and squirm. Our umbilical cord provides us nourishment and removes our waste. What a place to live!

However, one problem exists. We are sinful there from the moment of conception (Psalm 51:5). Enter Jesus! First, He, too, grew in a womb, living and moving as we did, but without sin. Then He takes our place on a cross, suffering and dying there with our sin. Then He takes our place in a tomb and destroys death by rising again.

When we leave our underwater womb world and are splashed in the waters of Baptism, we live underwater again! Baptism unites us with Jesus and all He did for us. "In Him we live and move and have our being" (Acts 17:28). We live surrounded by His mercy and grace. His "umbilical cord" of Word and Sacrament provides us nourishment and removes the waste of our sin through forgiveness. What a place to live!

But Luther reminds us that the work of Baptism continues. The perfect is yet to come! Baptized into Christ, we share in His resurrection. He gives new life now and the certain hope of our own resurrection on the Last Day. We will walk with Jesus in paradise. What a place to live . . . forever!

CLOSING PRAYER: Holy Spirit, thank You for uniting me with Jesus in the waters of Baptism. Help me live and move and have my being in Him. Strengthen me in my daily walk with Him. Whatever my circumstances may be, give me the hope of anticipating my eternal walk with Jesus. Amen.

Holy Baptism

Which are these words and promises of God?

Christ our Lord says in the last chapter of Mark: "Whoever believes and is baptized will be saved, but whoever does not believe will be condemned." (Mark 16:16)

———◦◦◦———

Jesus answered, "Truly, truly, I say to you, unless one is born of water and the Spirit, he cannot enter the kingdom of God." (John 3:5)

LUTHER'S WRITINGS ON HOLY BAPTISM

In the last chapter of Mark we read that "he who believes and is baptized will be saved" (Mark 16:16). And in this passage Christ declares that whoever is not born anew of the water and the Holy Spirit cannot come into the kingdom of God. Therefore God's words dare not be tampered with. Of course, we are well aware that Baptism is natural water. But after the Holy Spirit is added to it, we have more than mere water. It becomes a veritable bath of rejuvenation, a living bath which washes and purges man of sin and death, which cleanses him of all sin.

Christ wants to say: "You are not yet born anew. But I have come to bring you a new way of being born again, namely, a rebirth by water and the Holy Spirit, and to proclaim to you the necessity of this rebirth. I bring you a washing of regeneration which gives you a new birth and transforms you into a new person."

AE 22:283–84

Certainty in Christ's Promise — Jonathan Rusnak

Jesus took a basin, filled it with water, and began washing His disciples' feet. Peter resisted. "That's not for You to do, is it?" Why did Peter give in to Jesus? Jesus had told him, "If I do not wash you, you have no share with Me" (John 13:8). At that, Peter wanted a full-blown bath.

Jesus' words in Mark 16 seem less restrictive. Baptized believers will be saved. Unbelievers, not the unbaptized, will be condemned. If there is a loophole, it's for the sake of those who have not had the opportunity to receive Baptism in this life. They are not necessarily outside of God's grace in Christ. For everyone else, though, there is no other way to enter the kingdom of God (John 3:5). Like Peter, we must join Jesus at the font, where He promises to give us a share with Him (Romans 6:4–5).

Why does Jesus pinpoint Baptism as His saving washing? Above all, He does this for our benefit, that we would know, without a doubt, that when He washes us, He saves us (1 Peter 3:21). He gives what He promises. When we doubt this bath, we, like Peter, resist Jesus and His promised salvation.

Your baptismal certificate states the facts. Witnesses can attest to them. Maybe pictures prove them. There was a moment when Jesus washed you and gave you a share with Him. Faith holds on to Jesus' promises. You have been and will be saved. His promise is most certainly true.

——————— ⊸∘C⧓O∘⊷ ———————

CLOSING PRAYER: Dear Lord Jesus, You forgive, enliven, and save through Baptism. I resist You. Washed and cleansed from all sin, I doubt You and my standing before You. Rescued and made new, I return to my old ways of sin. Turn me back to the facts that I may trust Your promises for me. In Your name I pray. Amen.

Holy Baptism, Part 3

How can water do such great things?

Certainly not just the water, but the word of God in and with the water does these things, along with the faith which trusts this word of God in the water. For without God's word the water is plain water and no Baptism. But with the word of God it is a Baptism, that is, a life-giving water, rich in grace, and a washing of the new birth in the Holy Spirit, as St. Paul says in Titus, chapter three.

———— ∘⟡∘ ————

He saved us . . . by the washing of regeneration and renewal of the Holy Spirit, whom He poured out on us richly through Jesus Christ our Savior, so that being justified by His grace we might become heirs according to the hope of eternal life. The saying is trustworthy. (Titus 3:5–8)

LUTHER'S WRITINGS ON HOLY BAPTISM

We, too, say that an outward thing is nothing, if it is by itself; then it is utterly [without profit]. But if it is joined to the very will of God, then it does profit because of the will that has been attached to it. . . . Thus in Baptism there is not only mere water, because there is present here the name, or all the divine power joined through the Word in Baptism, and God Himself is the One who baptizes. Take note of this. But they do not listen, but stubbornly harp on the words: "An outward thing does not [do it]." Beware of their madness, because when an outward thing is grasped through the Word of God, it is a saving thing. If the humanity of Christ were without the Word, it would be a vain thing. But now we are saved through His blood and His body, because the Word is joined to it. Thus Baptism bears the Word of God by which the water is sanctified, and we are sanctified in the water.

AE 29:82

Am I Savable? — Heidi Goehmann

God baptizes. He holds you, me, infants, and adults in His arms and baptizes each believer in the water and with His Spirit. This is a miraculous picture! God is not absent, or else, as Luther writes, water would be "mere water"—nice, but not saving. Instead, God is fully present in His Word and with the water to bring salvation, grace, and life to us. He could stay in His heavens and be disconnected from us, but He does not. He could come to us in ways that would leave us guessing, "Is that God?" but He does not. Rather, He presents to us one very clear way to saving faith, and so we run, jump, and dance to be a part of it in His Church.

Who are the "theys" that do not listen? We are all "theys" to some degree. It is so easy to believe that simple water and the Bible are not enough, particularly when we look around us at a fallen world and inside of us, seeing our own brokenness. We wonder, "Am I savable?" In these times, we rest in the visible picture given to us in Titus 3: "He poured out on us richly through Jesus Christ our Savior" (v. 6). God is active. God pours salvation on us. This is more than enough to save. Paul says the words in Titus are "trustworthy," which means we are meant to repeat it to one another. God pours. God baptizes. God saves.

<hr>

CLOSING PRAYER: Lord, You are there at every Baptism, doing the action, using the hands of Your people to pour water onto our heads and into our souls. Lead us, tender Father, to remember the picture of You graciously saving us every day. In Jesus we pray. Amen.

Holy Baptism, Part 4

What does such baptizing with water indicate?

It indicates that the Old Adam in us should by daily contrition and repentance be drowned and die with all sins and evil desires, and that a new man should emerge and arise to live before God in righteousness and purity forever.

———∞◦⟋⟍◦∞———

We were buried therefore with Him by baptism into death, in order that, just as Christ was raised from the dead by the glory of the Father, we too might walk in newness of life. (Romans 6:4)

LUTHER'S WRITINGS ON HOLY BAPTISM

Thus the spiritual man, although he is present in all things with his senses, yet in his heart he is entirely withdrawn from these things and dead to all of them. This comes about when a man comes to hate all the things of this life from the very marrow of his bones. . . . But we must note that it is not necessary for all men to be found immediately in this state of perfection, as soon as they have been baptized into a death of this kind. For they are baptized "into death," that is, toward death, which is to say, they have begun to live in such a way that they are pursuing this kind of death and reach out toward this their goal. For although they are baptized into eternal life and the kingdom of heaven, yet they do not all at once possess this goal fully, but they have begun to act in such a way that they may attain to it—for Baptism was established to direct us toward death and through this death to life—therefore it is necessary that we come to it in the order which has been prescribed.

AE 25:312

The Old You and the New You — David Loy

God uses Baptism to wash away your sins. Whatever sins you have—past, present, and even future—were paid for when Jesus died on the cross, and in Baptism His sacrifice is applied to you. His blood covers you. His forgiveness is sufficient—more than sufficient—for you. There is not a sin in the world that Jesus did not pay for, and so there is not a sin in the world that Baptism does not wash away. In Baptism, you therefore die to the person you were—someone who did not love God and who loved him- or herself more than others. In Baptism, you receive the new life of a child of God. You become a coheir with Jesus of everlasting life. The Spirit fills you and moves you. You are a new creation, and in the power of the Holy Spirit, you begin to live as that new creation, that coheir of Jesus, that child of God.

Yet, as you well know, you are not yet the perfect child of God that you will be. There is only one remedy for the conflict between the old, dead, sinful you and the new, living, righteous you. Return to your Baptism. Repent of your sinfulness rather than embrace your sins. Tell God you are sorry. Remember that you are baptized and that your old, sinful self was put to death. And then, enlivened by the forgiveness that God gave you in Baptism, embrace the good works God's Spirit works in you.

CLOSING PRAYER: God of all grace, we thank You for the gift of Baptism. In it, You forgive our sins, make us Your dear children, and give us Your Holy Spirit. Grant that we who have received this gift may live each day in repentance and new life. In Jesus' name. Amen.

Confession

What is Confession?

Confession has two parts. First, that we confess our sins, and second, that we receive absolution, that is, forgiveness, from the pastor as from God Himself, not doubting, but firmly believing that by it our sins are forgiven before God in heaven.

—◦◦◦◦◦—

If we confess our sins, He is faithful and just to forgive us our sins and to cleanse us from all unrighteousness. (1 John 1:9)

LUTHER'S WRITINGS ON CONFESSION

Therefore if you believe the word of the priest when he absolves you . . . then your sins are assuredly absolved also before God, before all angels and all creatures—not for your sake, or for the priest's sake, but for the sake of the very Word of Christ, who cannot be lying to you when he says, "Whatever you loose . . . shall be loosed." Should you, however, not believe that your sins are truly forgiven and removed, then you are a heathen, acting toward your Lord Christ like one who is an unbeliever and not a Christian; and this is the most serious sin of all against God. Besides you had better not go to the priest if you will not believe his absolution; you will be doing yourself great harm by your disbelief. By such disbelief you make your God to be a liar when, through his priest, he says to you, "You are loosed from your sins," and you retort, "I don't believe it," or, "I doubt it." As if you were more certain in your opinion than God is in his words, whereas you should be letting personal opinions go, and with unshakeable faith giving place to the word of God spoken through the priest.   AE 35:13–14

A Little Too Personal — Heather Culli

The day's religion lesson had begun well. Twenty-one third graders eagerly filled a mural paper with all of the sins they could name in preparation for a discussion on forgiveness. They relished the opportunity to write about "bad stuff," and a mad rush of writing ensued. Brightly colored ink spelled out words like *lying*, *cheating*, *hitting*, *stealing*, *swearing*, even *murder*. The students were then asked to sit down and follow the directions on the board, which read,

> Think back on your day so far. Which of these sins have you committed today? Write each one on a sticky note and leave them on your desk until tomorrow.

The lesson hit a snag. There was no mad rush to fill the paper this time. Many sat in disbelief, while others flatly refused to comply. Even those who had begun writing sat hunched over, hiding their work with arms, hands, and torsos. One outspoken student shook her head and said, "This is just a little too personal." Directing them to our verse, the teacher pointed out that God promises forgiveness if we confess our sins. She went on to explain that God knows and loves us personally, so we can trust Him to hear our honest confession and forgive our sins.

In the act of confession, God does ask us to get personal. He expects us to be open and honest with Him and to trust that sincere confession leads to forgiveness. Each time we obey, God is quick to pour out His love and grace on the penitent sinner. Whether in private prayer or during a time of corporate Confession and Absolution, we can rest assured that God is faithful and just to forgive our sins and cleanse us from all unrighteousness.

———⟨∘⟨⟩∘⟩———

> CLOSING PRAYER: Dear Lord, thank You for the gift of Your Son, Jesus. It is through His death and resurrection that I am able to boldly come to You and personally confess my sin. With Your everlasting love, You keep Your promise to forgive my sin and remove it as far as the east is from the west. In Jesus' name I pray. Amen.

Confession

What sins should we confess?

Before God we should plead guilty of all sins, even those we are not aware of, as we do in the Lord's Prayer; but before the pastor we should confess only those sins which we know and feel in our hearts.

Who can discern his errors? Declare me innocent from hidden faults. (Psalm 19:12)

LUTHER'S WRITINGS ON CONFESSION

Therefore private confession is no place for [reciting] sins other than those which one openly recognizes as deadly, those which at the time are oppressing and frightening the conscience. For if one were to confess all his sins, he would have to be confessing every moment, since in this life we are never without sin. Even our good works are not pure and without sin. Yet it is not fruitless to confess the slighter sins, particularly if one is not aware of any mortal sins. For as has been said, in this sacrament God's word is heard, and [through it] faith is strengthened more and more. And even if one should have nothing to confess, it would still be profitable for the sake of that very faith to hear often the absolution, God's word. Thus one would grow accustomed to believing in the forgiveness of sins. This is why I said that the faith of the sacrament does everything, even though the confession be too much or too little. Everything is profitable to him who believes God's sacrament and word.

AE 35:20–21

"I'm So Sorry" — Scott Rauch

When we cross a line and harm our relationship with God and others, the punishment we deserve for this sinfulness is set aside because of Jesus' sacrifice. The Holy Spirit, in a wonderful and mysterious way, gives us faith and power to own up to who we are and what we do in our sinfulness. Confessing our sin and our sinful condition and expressing contrition (that's the "I'm sorry" part) is a statement of faith that we are not God and that we need His gracious love, mercy, and forgiveness.

It is hard, but so good, to hear words of confession from our own mouth and from the mouth and heart of someone who has hurt us. Relationships begin to be rebuilt when we truly own who we are as sinful people, accept and give the forgiveness of Jesus that is for us and lives through us, and then, through time and presence, truly understand what that forgiveness does for us.

This forgiveness sets aside what we are owed by God—eternal death and separation. This forgiveness is able to be given to us because Jesus took on what we are owed by God. His death, resurrection, and ascension together is the way He lives His rule and reign for our lives. We can confess who we are in Jesus because He makes us alive each day. The brokenness that we experience heals as we live in His love. Let us live in that well!

CLOSING PRAYER: Father, be merciful to me, a sinner. Let Your forgiveness through Jesus heal me, and let me be forgiving with those who have crossed the line with me. In Jesus. Amen.

The Office of the Keys

What is the Office of the Keys?

The Office of the Keys is that special authority which Christ has given to His church on earth to forgive the sins of repentant sinners, but to withhold forgiveness from the unrepentant as long as they do not repent.

―――――∽◦◦◇◦◦∽―――――

I will give you the keys of the kingdom of heaven, and whatever you bind on earth shall be bound in heaven, and whatever you loose on earth shall be loosed in heaven. (Matthew 16:19)

LUTHER'S WRITINGS ON THE OFFICE OF THE KEYS

He binds and joins himself to our work. Indeed, he himself commands us to do his own work. Why then, should we make it uncertain or reverse it, pretending he must first bind and loose in heaven? Just as if his binding and loosing in heaven were different from our binding and loosing on earth. Or, as if he had different keys in heaven above from those we have below on earth. He distinctly and clearly states that they are heaven's keys and not those of the earth. You shall have my keys (he says), and no others. And you shall have them here on earth. Clearly above and besides these keys of heaven, he can have no others which are not to be used in heaven, but above and outside of heaven. What would they bind there? If now they are the keys of heaven, then they are not of two kinds but of one kind only, binding and loosing here on earth and in heaven above.

AE 40:365

Freeing the Captives — Faith Spelbring

The Pirates of the Caribbean attraction at Disneyland guides visitors through a pirate's life as they drift down a stream on the boat ride. One scene depicts prisoners in a jail, calling for a stray dog to come over to their cell. The dog just so happens to be holding the keys to their cell in his teeth. Dangling a bone through the bars of the cell, the prisoners know that the dog possesses the keys that will set them free.

While most people have not been locked behind bars, we have all been in chains that bind us. In Romans 6:17–23, Paul described us as once slaves to sin but now set free because of Jesus. Our sin separates us from God and from others, but Jesus' work of salvation on our behalf opens the prison and sets us captives free, just as the prophet foretold in Isaiah 61.

The power to forgive sins is God's alone, but He entrusted His Church with His authority and power to bind and loosen the sinner's chains, saying, "Whatever you bind on earth shall be bound in heaven, and whatever you loose on earth shall be loosed in heaven."

Perhaps it is because God created us as relational beings that our churches call pastors to hear our confession and, by God's authority and because of Jesus' death on the cross, look us square in the eye to specifically tell us our sins are forgiven and proclaim liberty to the captives.

⌐∘∘◦∘⌐

CLOSING PRAYER: God of freedom, thank You for loosening our sinful chains through Christ, who is the Key. You've given Your Church responsibility to bind and loosen on earth and in heaven. Give her wisdom to know what is right and courage to do it. We pray this in Jesus' name. Amen.

The Office of the Keys

What do you believe according to these words?

I believe that when the called ministers of Christ deal
with us by His divine command, in particular when they
exclude openly unrepentant sinners from the Christian
congregation and absolve those who repent of their sins
and want to do better, this is just as valid and certain, even
in heaven, as if Christ our dear Lord dealt with us Himself.

⟡

And when He had said this, He breathed on them and
said to them, "Receive the Holy Spirit. If you forgive
the sins of any, they are forgiven them; if you withhold
forgiveness from any, it is withheld." (John 20:22–23)

LUTHER'S WRITINGS ON THE OFFICE OF THE KEYS

The key which binds is the power or office to punish the sinner who refuses to repent by means of a public condemnation to eternal death and
separation from the rest of Christendom. And when such a judgment is
pronounced, it is a judgment of Christ himself. And if the sinner perseveres
in his sin, he is certainly eternally damned. The loosing key is the power or office to absolve the sinner who makes confession and is converted
from sins, promising again eternal life. And it has the same significance
as if Christ himself passed judgment. And if he believes and continues in
this faith he is certainly saved forever. For the key which binds carries
forward the work of the law. It is profitable to the sinner inasmuch as it
reveals to him his sins, admonishes him to fear God, causes him to trem-
ble, and moves him to repentance, and not to destruction. The loosing key
carries forward the work of the gospel. It invites to grace and mercy. It
comforts and promises life and salvation through the forgiveness of sins.

In short, the two keys advance and foster the gospel by simply proclaiming these two things: repentance and forgiveness of sins [Luke 24:47].

AE 40:372–73

The Two Keys and Me — Jonathan Boehne

We know that Jesus has given two keys for the door of heaven. One key locks the door shut. The other key opens the door. Sometimes, as a Christian, I need the key that locks the door shut to me. I need to see the true severity of my sin. I may think the door is open to me, even though I continue in my sin without any concern for God's Law. This is the binding key. It binds my sin until I turn to Jesus. And it's good for me because it shows me my evil and calls me to faith.

Other times, I need only the key that opens the door of heaven. This is the best and most comforting key. In my guilt and shame, I imagine that the door to heaven is closed to me and will never be opened again. Yet I confess my sin to Jesus and beg for mercy. And I hear the sweetest sound of heaven's doors swinging open to me in these words, "By the command of Christ, I forgive you all your sins." And I know that when a called pastor of the Church deals with me in this way, it's just as true and certain as if Jesus Himself dealt with me.

This is how my good and faithful pastor Jesus Christ loves me and cares for me. He uses these keys to keep me on the middle road between prideful arrogance and hopeless despair. He walks me down that road of humble and joyful faith into the open doors of heaven.

———⊸o⪜⪝o⊶———

CLOSING PRAYER: Father, You know my sin and my need for forgiveness. Give me comfort in the Keys that Jesus has given to His Church. Bring me always to repentance, to joyful faith, and to the forgiveness of all my sins. Through Jesus Christ, our Lord. Amen.

The Priesthood of All Believers

But you are a chosen race, a royal priesthood, a holy nation, a people for His own possession, that you may proclaim the excellencies of Him who called you out of darkness into His marvelous light. (1 Peter 2:9)

—◦◦◦◦—

Let the word of Christ dwell in you richly, teaching and admonishing one another in all wisdom, singing psalms and hymns and spiritual songs, with thankfulness in your hearts to God. (Colossians 3:16)

LUTHER'S WRITINGS ON THE PRIESTHOOD OF ALL BELIEVERS

But after we have become Christians through this Priest and His priestly office, incorporated in Him by Baptism through faith, then each one, according to his calling and position, obtains the right and the power of teaching and confessing before others this Word which we have obtained from Him. Even though not everybody has the public office and calling, every Christian has the right and the duty to teach, instruct, admonish, comfort, and rebuke his neighbor with the Word of God at every opportunity and whenever necessary. For example, father and mother should do this for their children and household; a brother, neighbor, citizen, or peasant for the other. Certainly one Christian may instruct and admonish another ignorant or weak Christian concerning the Ten Commandments, the Creed, or the Lord's Prayer. And he who receives such instruction is also under obligation to accept it as God's Word and publicly to confess it.

AE 13:333

Yes, Indeed, a Right and a Privilege — Philip Rigdon

A change takes place in children at roughly age 9 or 10. Prior to this change, children will respond to a teacher's request with enthusiasm. "Who would like to erase the whiteboard?" "Pick me! Pick me!" As children pass into adolescence, they respond to the same request with sullen reservation. What was once a privilege is suddenly a burden. Christians often respond in a similar fashion to God's call to, as Luther writes, "teach, instruct, admonish, comfort, and rebuke." Review the Scripture and Luther's passage here. Far from an onerous liability, telling others about Jesus as part of the priesthood of all believers is described as a consummate joy! Peter writes that we are chosen, royal, and holy. Luther explains that we are given a right and a power.

So it is! Chosen, we recognize that God stepped forward to rescue us from sin and darkness. We receive the benefits of His saving work. God made us royal and holy as a reflection, not of who we are, but rather of who our Lord and Savior, Jesus Christ, is. The King of heaven came into the world to save sinners. Through His suffering and death, Jesus earned our forgiveness. God's Holy Spirit brings that forgiveness to us through faith, setting us apart, making us holy and ready for heaven. There is no title more precious than Christian, and no message more important than salvation in Jesus—and God has given His priests the right and power to share it.

———— ∘◦◦◦◦∘ ————

CLOSING PRAYER: Dear redeeming and saving Lord, inspire us by Your Spirit to embrace our priesthood, not as a burden, but as the privilege and joy it is. As You have chosen and made us holy in Christ, use us as You will to further Your kingdom. In Your name we pray. Amen.

The Office of the Public Ministry

Christ has instituted the pastoral office through which the Office of the Keys is exercised publicly, that is, on behalf of the Church. The Christian congregation, acting in accordance with the will of Christ, calls qualified men to serve as His ministers, forgiving and retaining sins according to His command. (SC, Question 343)

———————⟡———————

And He gave the apostles, the prophets, the evangelists, the shepherds and teachers. (Ephesians 4:11)

Jesus said to them again, "Peace be with you. As the Father has sent Me, even so I am sending you." (John 20:21)

LUTHER'S WRITINGS ON THE OFFICE OF THE PUBLIC MINISTRY

The other sending is, of course, also of God; but it is done through men and means, since the office of preaching and of the use of the power of the keys was established by God. This office will remain, and there will be no other preaching office. But the persons do not remain; they die. Therefore we must always have new preachers; and this does not happen without means. The office as such, that is, the Word of God, Baptism, and the Lord's Supper, come directly from Christ; but after that Christ is no longer on earth. So there is a different sending, which is *by* men though not *of* men. Thus *we* are sent, and we also elect others and put them into office in order to preach and administer the Sacraments. Yet this sending is also of God; for God has commanded it, and though we help, God Himself sends laborers into His vineyard, though He does it through men.

WLS § 2967

Who's in Charge? — James Lamb

"Who's in charge here?" The principal may ask that question on entering an overly noisy classroom. The teacher appears to be teaching, but the students do not appear to be learning. They talk and giggle and disrupt. Who's in charge?

The question may come up in Lutheran congregations as well. Who's in charge? Is it the pastor? He is a highly trained theologian. He received a certificate of ordination. He knows the biblical languages. He preaches, teaches, baptizes, consecrates, marries, and buries.

Or is it the congregation? They called the pastor. They pay his salary and provide him housing and health insurance. They make important decisions in voters' meetings. They elect leaders and establish boards and committees.

Who's in charge, the pastor or the congregation? Neither! Christ is in charge! It is His church. However, He works through people to accomplish His will for His church. He calls men into the Office of the Public Ministry, yet He does so through the congregation. He gives His pastors authority to forgive and retain sins, but He gives it through His people in a local congregation.

Think of the harmony that would prevail in congregations when we all acknowledge who is actually in charge! Members would respect their pastor as the undershepherd of the Good Shepherd, sent to minister to them. Pastors would respect their members as the sheep of Christ's pasture to love and nurture as Christ Himself does.

So, pastors, relax. Laypeople, relax. Christ is in charge! Joyfully serve Him together.

———— ∽◦◦◦∽ ————

CLOSING PRAYER: Lord of the Church, thank You for sending faithful pastors to shepherd Your people. Continue to raise up men for the Office of the Public Ministry. Thank You for faithful laypeople through whom You call men to this office. Unite us all to serve You, the one in charge. In Your name we pray. Amen.

The Sacrament of the Altar

What is the Sacrament of the Altar?

It is the true body and blood of our Lord Jesus Christ under the bread and wine, instituted by Christ Himself for us Christians to eat and to drink.

<hr>

For I received from the Lord what I also delivered to you, that the Lord Jesus on the night when He was betrayed took bread, and when He had given thanks, He broke it, and said, "This is My body, which is for you. Do this in remembrance of Me." In the same way also He took the cup, after supper, saying, "This cup is the new covenant in My blood. Do this, as often as you drink it, in remembrance of Me." (1 Corinthians 11:23–25)

LUTHER'S WRITINGS ON THE SACRAMENT OF THE ALTAR

Here, too, out of two kinds of objects a union has taken place, which I shall call a "sacramental union," because Christ's body and the bread are given to us as a sacrament. . . .

Therefore, it is entirely correct to say, if one points to the bread, "This is Christ's body," and whoever sees the bread sees Christ's body, as John says that he saw the Holy Spirit when he saw the dove, as we have heard. Thus also it is correct to say, "He who takes hold of this bread, takes hold of Christ's body; and he who eats this bread, eats Christ's body; he who crushes this bread with teeth or tongue, crushes with teeth or tongue the body of Christ." And yet it remains absolutely true that no one sees or grasps or eats or chews Christ's body in the way he visibly sees and chews any other flesh. What one does to the bread is rightly and properly attributed to the body of Christ by virtue of the sacramental union.

AE 37:300

Real Presence — Jonathan Rusnak

We call it "real presence." It's no representation. It's His body and blood in, with, and under bread and wine. We take Jesus at His Word.

Preoccupied by sacramental logistics, however, it's possible to miss the point. *Jesus* is there! *He* is present and active there for you. You take Him at His Word, but you take *Him*! Risen and reigning, He returns through a meal to deliver to you the fruits of His cross: the body and blood, broken and shed then and there but given to you to receive here and now.

So, before He accomplishes anything else, He establishes His presence. He gives you new eyes of faith to see with your ears, to wonder and marvel at His way of coming to you in such a humble way, and to trust that, through the bread and wine you consume, He enters as Lord and Savior.

Not everyone received Jesus in His ministry (John 1:11). Many did. Receiving Jesus means receiving His presence, His Word, His work, and His gifts. Wherever He is, that's where the kingdom of God is, that's where the Church is, that's where heaven is (Matthew 4:17)! Not only that, but every Christian receives the same Jesus; in Him the Church has its unity (1 John 1:1–10).

Jesus, really present, continues to teach you to receive Him (Hebrews 5:14). He teaches you to see with your ears and trust His Word. Best of all, He promises to receive you at His heavenly table (Luke 22:30).

CLOSING PRAYER: Dear Lord Jesus, You give Your Supper, and in Your Supper You give me Yourself, Your body and blood for me to eat and drink. Send Your Spirit and give me faith to receive You as You come to me that I might receive You and all the eternal gifts You desire to give me. In Your name I pray. Amen.

The Sacrament of the Altar

What is the benefit of this eating and drinking?

These words, "Given and shed for you for the forgiveness of sins," show us that in the Sacrament forgiveness of sins, life, and salvation are given us through these words. For where there is forgiveness of sins, there is also life and salvation.

———⊸∘⟋⟍∘⊶———

In Him we have redemption through His blood, the forgiveness of our trespasses, according to the riches of His grace. (Ephesians 1:7)

Luther's Writings on the Sacrament of the Altar

For this reason every Christian must know these words, letter for letter: "Here my Lord has given me his body and blood in the bread and wine, in order that I should eat and drink. And they are to be my very own, so that I may be certain that my sins are forgiven, that I am to be free of death and hell, have eternal life, and be a child of God and an heir of heaven. Therefore I go to the sacrament to seek these things. I am a poor sinner with death before me, I must go through it; and the devil threatens me with all kinds of trouble and danger. Because I am in sin, a captive of death and the devil, because I feel that I am weak in faith, cold in love, wayward, impatient, envious, with sin clinging to me before and behind; therefore I come hither where I find and hear Christ's word that I shall receive the gift of forgiveness of sins."

AE 36:350

Inside-Out Grace — Heidi Goehmann

Living inside of redemption, surrounded by the richness of God's grace, is exactly what the Lord's Supper is about. God leaves the tangible for us because He knows that the devil indeed threatens, trouble and danger do assail, love is cold on this earth, and sin clings tightly to us in word and deed. Taking the body and blood of Christ in the bread and wine physically places forgiveness into every system in our bodies, filling us from the inside out with the love of Christ, the mercy of Christ, and the heart of Christ. We can certainly have forgiveness in Christ apart from the Lord's Supper, but I also wouldn't want to miss out on this inside-out grace of my Savior. I "come hither" because God the Father is inviting me. God wants my company. God wants to fill me. God meets with me.

Can you imagine living outside of that knowledge? Can you imagine wondering whether God would receive you? This is the reality for many in our world. In the message of the Lord's Supper, we share with them also the message of freedom in Christ, the love of Christ, and the strength of Christ. We go out with the Supper in us, messengers of life and salvation. Because we are filled, we may overflow with words and actions, not of death and condemnation, but of life and salvation. I seek God at the Sacrament, knowing I am welcome. I share God in the world, knowing sinners are welcome.

―――――∽◦⬯◦∾―――――

CLOSING PRAYER: Lord, You fill us with Your mercy and kindness. Help us to know that we are invited by You, because You have slain death and the devil. Silence our fears between each Supper. Ignite our hearts through Your Spirit to leave the Table, ready to share Your goodness. In Christ we pray. Amen.

The Sacrament of the Altar

How can bodily eating and drinking do such great things?

Certainly not just eating and drinking do these things, but the words written here: "Given and shed for you for the forgiveness of sins." These words, along with the bodily eating and drinking, are the main thing in the Sacrament. Whoever believes these words has exactly what they say: "forgiveness of sins."

⧫

Heaven and earth will pass away, but My words will not pass away. (Matthew 24:35)

LUTHER'S WRITINGS ON THE SACRAMENT OF THE ALTAR

See, then, what a beautiful, great, marvelous thing this is, how everything meshes together in one sacramental reality. The words are the first thing, for without the words the cup and the bread would be nothing. Further, without bread and cup, the body and blood of Christ would not be there. Without the body and blood of Christ, the new testament would not be there. Without the new testament, forgiveness of sins would not be there. Without forgiveness of sins, life and salvation would not be there. Thus the words first connect the bread and the cup to the sacrament; bread and cup embrace the body and blood of Christ; body and blood of Christ embrace the new testament; the new testament embraces the forgiveness of sins; forgiveness of sins embraces eternal life and salvation. See, all this the words of the Supper offer and give us, and we embrace it by faith.

AE 37:338

The Power of God's Word — David Loy

When God speaks, things happen. When there was nothing at all besides Him, He said, "'Let there be light,' and there was light" (Genesis 1:3). Through the angel Gabriel, He told the Virgin Mary that she would conceive and bear a Son, and she did. Through apostles and prophets and pastors and parents and grandparents and neighbors, He shares the Good News of Jesus' death and resurrection, and people come to faith. His Word does what it says because His Word has the power to create.

That is how something as simple and ordinary as eating a bit of bread and drinking a sip of wine can give you forgiveness of sins, life, and salvation. When our Lord Jesus invites you to His Table and blesses the bread and wine with His Word, you receive His body and blood for the forgiveness of your sins. No other human's word could do that. No parent or grandparent, no pastor or priest can make bread and wine into Christ's body and blood, much less bless you with forgiveness on the authority of his own words. Our Lord, however, is not just any other human being. He is also true God with the Father and the Spirit. His Word brought creation into being at the beginning. His Word turned water into wine at Cana. His Word healed the sick and raised the dead. His Word unites His body and blood with bread and wine, through which you receive forgiveness, life, and salvation.

CLOSING PRAYER: Almighty God, we thank You for the Lord's Supper. Sustain us in the true faith, so that we trust Jesus' powerful Word, which makes ordinary bread and wine into His body and blood, and so that we receive the forgiveness, life, and salvation You have promised. In His name. Amen.

The Sacrament of the Altar

Who receives this sacrament worthily?

Fasting and bodily preparation are certainly fine outward training. But that person is truly worthy and well prepared who has faith in these words: "Given and shed for you for the forgiveness of sins." But anyone who does not believe these words or doubts them is unworthy and unprepared, for the words "for you" require all hearts to believe.

———⌾———

Those who are well have no need of a physician, but those who are sick. (Matthew 9:12)

LUTHER'S WRITINGS ON THE SACRAMENT OF THE ALTAR

Such people must learn that it is the highest art to know that our Sacrament does not depend upon our worthiness. We are not baptized because we are worthy and holy. Nor do we go to Confession because we are pure and without sin. On the contrary, we go because we are poor, miserable people. We go exactly because we are unworthy. This is true unless we are talking about someone who desires no grace and Absolution nor intends to change.

But whoever would gladly receive grace and comfort should drive himself and allow no one to frighten him away. Say, "I, indeed would like to be worthy. But I come, not upon any worthiness, but upon Your Word, because You have commanded it. I come as one who would gladly be Your disciple, no matter what becomes of my worthiness." This is difficult. We always have this obstacle and hindrance to encounter: we look more upon ourselves than upon Christ's Word and lips. For human nature desires to act in such a way that it can stand and rest firmly on itself. Otherwise, it refuses to approach.

LC V 61–63

Urgent Care — Heather Culli

As a parent, I have logged my fair share of time at urgent care. There is always plenty of time to indulge in my favorite pastime, people-watching. One thing I've observed is that everyone in the waiting room is either sick or injured. Unlike a typical physician's office, there are no services for healthy people. Urgent care offers no wellness checks, vaccinations, or sports physicals. Those who come are in need. They've come seeking prompt attention, diagnosis, and relief.

In many ways, this is a fitting metaphor for the Sacrament of the Altar. In our verse above, Jesus compares Himself to a physician, saying that it is the sick who need Him rather than the healthy. Repentant sinners are welcome at the altar. They have acknowledged the infection of sin in their lives and have expressed their need for relief in Jesus' name. Their confession is sincere, and their desire for grace is true. However, no place is found for the self-righteous, those who think God's forgiveness is theirs without the blood of Jesus. Pride such as this fools sinners into the fallacy of self-sufficiency. As Luther states, "We look more upon ourselves than upon Christ's Word."

Turning our gaze to the cross forces us to examine our own unworthiness in the light of Jesus' sacrifice. Realizing and confessing that His blood was shed for you and your forgiveness makes you truly worthy of the Sacrament. Our Great Physician is quick to comfort and relieve hearts that believe. No appointment necessary!

∞◦⌒◦∞

> CLOSING PRAYER: Dear God, You sent Your only Son into the world to save sinners. Stir up Your truth in our hearts to recognize our need for a Savior. Forgive us when we look more upon ourselves than Your Word. Bring us regularly to the altar to receive the forgiveness given to us by Christ Jesus. In Your name we pray. Amen.

Table of Duties

The catechism concludes with the Table of Duties—a listing of Bible passages addressing the very down-to-earth and yet high and holy callings of Christians in their daily lives. It is modeled after the listing of household responsibilities in Colossians 3:8–4:1 and Ephesians 5:22–6:9. It is Luther's way of applying the catechism to daily life. The list of Bible passages is arranged under three general headings: (1) life in the congregation; (2) life in the civic community; and (3) life in the household. (Explanation, "Table of Duties")

As each has received a gift, use it to serve one another, as good stewards of God's varied grace: whoever speaks, as one who speaks oracles of God; whoever serves, as one who serves by the strength that God supplies—in order that in everything God may be glorified through Jesus Christ. (1 Peter 4:10–11)

Luther's Writings on the Table of Duties

There the will of the Groom is that He alone should speak, and the Bride [is] to listen to nothing other than the Groom. This serves so that the neighbor is helped and God is praised. For when I preach in such a way that you understand the Word of God, [then] I am unable to have dominion over you, [nor are you able] to be subjected to me. . . . Thus learn that in the Church nothing other than the Word of God shall be heard. Elsewhere there is land, people, house, [and] court where you can have your fill of speaking, each one according to his own station—so long as one does not bring that filth into the Church. There the Word of God alone [has its place]. There [in the Church] remains the praise of God and the well-being of the neighbor. There you do not give thanks to me; the honor goes to whom it is owed, to the Father through Christ. Then give thanks and remunerate, for what [I have] faithfully preached and you have heard.

AE 57:347

The Vocation of Christians Together — Scott Rauch

The rhythms of our living are influenced and directed by the Father through Jesus by the power of the Holy Spirit. Reading, praying, speaking, thinking about, singing, and living in the Word of God, who is Jesus, will weave His love, grace, mercy, and justice in every single thing we say and do throughout our entire day.

As we gather as God's people, in large groups and in smaller ones, we hear what God speaks to us as people together. We get the opportunity to hear God's Word together and listen to and challenge one another. We get to play, eat, and enjoy life together. Christ's Church, His Body, in all the ways it is expressed locally, is given the gift of shining the light and love of Jesus in practical, creative, and ongoing ways.

As the family of God together, we each have our job, calling, and responsibility in His family. It is a grind. It is such hard work. It is monotonous, ritualistic, and rote, and at the same time it is joyful, celebrative, and surprising. And that's why it is best done together, never alone. But Jesus does not depend on us to do it alone. He, along with His Father and the Holy Spirit, does it right with us. It is His vocation with us. And we get to do ours with Him. What joy this is!

CLOSING PRAYER: Almighty God, in Your vocation of Creator, Savior, and Lord and Giver of life, You faithfully make us family. May we imitate You as we create, love, and live in our vocational living together. In Jesus' name. Amen.

Table of Duties

In the civic community, we live as citizens with responsibility to the government. (Explanation, "Table of Duties")

⸻

Let every person be subject to the governing authorities. For there is no authority except from God, and those that exist have been instituted by God. (Romans 13:1)

LUTHER'S WRITINGS ON THE TABLE OF DUTIES

Nevertheless, worldly government is a glorious ordinance and splendid gift of God, who has instituted and established it and will have it maintained as something men cannot do without. If there were no worldly government, one man could not stand before another; each would necessarily devour the other, as irrational beasts devour one another. Therefore as it is the function and honor of the office of preaching to make sinners saints, dead men live, damned men saved, and the devil's children God's children, so it is the function and honor of worldly government to make men out of wild beasts and to prevent men from becoming wild beasts. . . . Protection of this sort does not exist among the beasts, and if it were not for worldly government there would be none of it among men either; they would surely cease to be men and become mere beasts.

AE 46:237–38

Rescued from the Lord of the Flies — Faith Spelbring

William Golding's novel *Lord of the Flies* portrays a gruesome picture of what happens when civil order is lost and the beast that lurks within man is not kept at bay. After their plane crashes, boys are stranded on an island. Two leaders arise, Ralph and Jack, who vie for power. As the story unfolds, friends turn on one another, the worst in people is exposed, and "littluns" live out their worst nightmares.

Golding wasn't the first to reveal this side of human nature. Some four hundred years earlier, Martin Luther wrote, "It is the function and honor of worldly government to make men out of wild beasts and to prevent men from becoming wild beasts."

God has given us governing authorities to keep order in His world. How well this is carried out by those in office may vary, but their job is to protect their people from dangers—foreign and domestic.

In *Lord of the Flies*, Jack sets a fire intended to kill Ralph. The fire ends up signaling a naval ship and the boys are rescued. What was intended to kill actually rescued.

When we fail to repress the beast within, when leaders fail to protect those in their charge, when we resemble beasts more than the One in whose image we were created, we can take heart in the cross. The cross was intended to kill, but through the death of Jesus on the cross, we are rescued from the beasts—foreign and domestic—of sin, death, and the devil.

———— ◦◦◦◦ ————

CLOSING PRAYER: Ruler of every nation, on our own, we are dangerous to others and ourselves. Thank You for giving us leaders and laws to instruct and guide us. Forgive us when we cannot tame our inner beast or trust in those You put in charge. Teach us, Lord, to obey. Amen.

Table of Duties

In the household, the family lives together according to God's design. Husbands are to treat their wives with honor and love (1 Peter 3:7; Colossians 3:19).

Wives are to submit to their husbands as to the Lord (Ephesians 5:22; 1 Peter 3:5–6).

Parents are to be gentle with their children, instructing them in the Christian faith (Ephesians 6:4). (Explanation, "Table of Duties")

———◦◦◦◦———

Train up a child in the way he should go; even when he is old he will not depart from it. (Proverbs 22:6)

Luther's Writings on the Table of Duties

Third, [the doctors say] that marriage produces offspring, for that is the end and chief purpose of marriage. It is not enough, however, merely for children to be born, and so what they say about marriage excusing sin does not apply in this case. Heathen, too, bear offspring. But unfortunately it seldom happens that we bring up children to serve God, to praise and honor him, and want nothing else of them. People seek only heirs in their children, or pleasure in them; the serving of God finds what place it can. You also see people rush into marriage and become mothers and fathers before they know what the commandments are or can pray. . . . False natural love blinds parents so that they have more regard for the bodies of their children than they have for their souls. . . . Therefore, it is of the greatest importance for every married man to pay closer, more thorough, and continuous attention to the health of his child's soul than to the body which he has begotten, and to regard his child as nothing else but an eternal treasure God has commanded him to protect, and so prevent the world, the flesh, and the devil from stealing the child away and bringing him to destruction.   AE 44:12, 13

The Family To-Do List — Jonathan Boehne

More than a few family refrigerators have displayed, next to pictures and artwork and shopping lists, a list of chores. Everybody in the family is expected to contribute and do their part. That's being a family — loving and serving one another. It's our duty, even if that means cleaning a bathroom or doing the dishes.

The same is true for children of the heavenly Father. In His family, we love and serve one another. In the Catechism, Luther gave God's list of "chores," which he called the Table of Duties. They remind us that our primary question should be not "What's my family supposed to do for me?" but rather "What does God command me to do for my family?"

For parents, God says our duty is to be gentle with our children and teach them God's Word to save their souls. For children, God commands us to honor our parents. For husbands, God gives us the duty of loving our wives and caring for them. And for wives, God says our duty is loving and respecting our husbands.

The strength to serve our earthly family is found in our heavenly family. God our Father loves and cares for us. Jesus, our Brother and the husband of the Church, covers us with grace. And the Holy Spirit, our Comforter, works through the Word of God to give us faith. Our triune God promises to be with us as we fulfill the duties He gives us as wives, husbands, children, and parents.

—◦◦⟳◦◦—

CLOSING PRAYER: Father in heaven, You command us to love, honor, and respect our wives, husbands, children, and parents. Forgive us when we shirk our duties, and renew our desire to love and serve others just as You, Father, Son, and Holy Spirit, have loved and served us. Through Jesus Christ, our Lord. Amen.

Christian Questions

After confession and instruction in the Ten Commandments, the Creed, the Lord's Prayer, and the Sacraments of Baptism and the Lord's Supper, the pastor may ask or Christians may ask themselves, these questions. (Introduction to Christian Questions with Their Answers)

∞◦⟨∽⟩◦∞

Let a person examine himself, then, and so eat of the bread and drink of the cup. (1 Corinthians 11:28)

LUTHER'S WRITINGS ON CHRISTIAN QUESTIONS

They have interpreted this saying to mean that we should examine our consciences for sin, although it means rather that we should examine ourselves for faith and trust, since no man can discover all his mortal sins, as has been shown above from Ps. 19[:12], "Lord, who knows his sin?" Moreover, not to be conscious of mortal sin is not enough, for St. Paul says in 1 Cor. [4:4], "I am not aware of anything against myself, but I am not thereby acquitted." Why then do they drive us into such impossible, futile, and worthless works and why do they conceal the very faith for which a man ought to scrutinize or examine himself most of all? As was said under the previous article, they are always trying to drive us away from faith and into works; I wish we would be driven away from works and into faith, for the works will surely follow faith, but faith never follows works.

AE 32:55

Let the Mystery Be a Mystery — Philip Rigdon

Do you keep an extra house key hidden underneath a rock, planter, or garden gnome in the front yard? Your home is secure only until someone overturns that stone. Some stones were not meant to be overturned. Some doors were not meant to be opened—at least, not yet. Many of the greatest errors in Christian teaching have been a result of manufacturing answers when God is silent. How can bread and wine also be the very body and blood of our Savior, Jesus Christ? No one on earth understands how, and only through faith do we believe it. Much Christian frustration has its roots in looking for evidence in the wrong places. As Luther explains above, we imagine that a full accounting of sin is sufficient evidence of preparedness for Holy Communion. An adequate number of good works will prove that I am ready to receive Christ in this Supper.

Why should we be surprised to find that we doubt Holy Communion? Without the work of the Holy Spirit, we would not trust in Christ! Therefore, be comforted. Our heavenly Father knows that we struggle and doubt. Doubt in Holy Communion need not suggest that it is false, but rather that saints are still sinners. Cry out to the Lord, "Help my unbelief!" He will do so. He will cast away doubt and fortify the faith He created. He will do so because He wants you to have the benefits of His work on the cross—forgiveness of sins and life eternal.

CLOSING PRAYER: Dear Lord, protect me from the temptation to manufacture my own answers where Your Word is silent. When I struggle to trust in You and Your Sacraments, drown my doubt and revive my faith. Point me ever to Your goodness and mercy shown in Christ, Your Word, and the Sacraments. In Your name we pray. Amen.

Christian Questions

What should we do when we eat His body and drink His blood, and in this way receive His pledge?

We should remember and proclaim His death and the shedding of His blood, as He taught us. This do, as often as you drink it, in remembrance of Me.

————— ◦◦◦◦◦ —————

Immediately the father of the child cried out and said, "I believe; help my unbelief!" (Mark 9:24)

Luther's Writings on Christian Questions

Now, this is to be the first point, especially for those who are cold and indifferent. Then they may reflect upon it and rouse themselves. For this is certainly true, as I have found in my own experience, and as everyone will find in his own case: if a person withdraws like this from the Sacrament, he will daily become more and more callous and cold, and will at last disregard the Sacrament completely. To avoid this, we must examine our heart and conscience [1 Corinthians 11:28; 2 Corinthians 13:5], and we must act like people who desire to be right with God [Psalm 78:37]. The more this is done, the more the heart will be warmed and enkindled, so it may not become entirely cold.

But if you say, "How can I come if I feel that I am not prepared?" Answer, "That is also my cause for hesitation, especially because of the old way under the pope." At that time we tortured ourselves to be so perfectly pure that God could not find the least blemish in us. . . . If you consider how good and pure you are and labor to have no hesitations, you would never approach.

LC V 53–55, 57

Open-Book Exam — James Lamb

Most people do not like exams. Although if the instructor says, "This will be an open-book exam," that relieves some stress. Luther's Christian Questions can be compared to an open-book exam, and the open book is the Bible.

As in the classroom, we learn things when we take this exam. First, like the father of the demon-possessed boy in Mark 9:24, we learn we need help with our unbelief. The answers we find in our open book tell us of our sinfulness. They remind us that we break God's commands and deserve His punishment. Every time we sin, our unbelief shows through. We find ourselves helpless and can only beg, "Help my unbelief!"

The second thing we learn in our open-book exam is that God loves us, unbelief and all. By grace and through the power of His Holy Spirit, He enables us to believe in Jesus as the only hope for our unbelief. Like the father in Mark 9, we can also cry out, "I believe." We believe in all that God has done in Christ to bring us forgiveness, life, and salvation.

What we learn in our open-book exam about our unbelief and our belief impels us to come to the Sacrament of our Savior's body and blood. There we find our beggarly prayer for help answered through the forgiveness of sins. There we find renewal of our belief so that it may have more power over our unbelief as we live our lives as Christ's people.

CLOSING PRAYER: Lord Jesus, thank You for teaching us as we examine ourselves based on Your Word of truth. Every day, and especially when we approach Your Holy Supper, we ask You, as that father did long ago, "I believe; help my unbelief." Amen.

Luther's Seal

He is the image of the invisible God, the firstborn of all creation. (Colossians 1:15)

LUTHER'S WRITINGS ON LUTHER'S SEAL

Honorable, kind, dear Sir and Friend! Since you ask whether my seal has come out correctly, I shall answer most amiably and tell you of those thoughts which [now] come to my mind about my seal as a symbol of my theology.

There is first to be a cross, black [and placed] in a heart, which should be of its natural color, so that I myself would be reminded that faith in the Crucified saves us. For if one believes from the heart he will be justified. Even though it is a black cross, [which] mortifies and [which] also should hurt us, yet it leaves the heart in its [natural] color [and] does not ruin nature; that is, [the cross] does not kill but keeps [man] alive. For the just man lives by faith, but by faith in the Crucified One. Such a heart is to be in the midst of a white rose, to symbolize that faith gives joy, comfort, and peace; in a word it places the believer into a white joyful rose; for [this faith] does not give peace and joy as the world gives and, therefore, the rose is to be white and not red, for white is the color of the spirits and of all the angels. Such a rose is to be in a sky-blue field, [symbolizing] that such joy in the Spirit and in faith is a beginning of the future heavenly joy; it is already a part [of faith], and is grasped through hope, even though not yet manifest. And around this field is a golden ring, [symbolizing] that in heaven such blessedness lasts forever and has no end, and in addition is precious beyond all joy and goods, just as gold is the most valuable and precious metal.

AE 49:358–59

A Simple Summary — Jonathan Rusnak

When it comes right down to it, the Christian faith is simple. That, after all, is the goal of the catechism: to present the deep spiritual truths of Scripture in a way even a child can grasp. I will never grow out of my need for simple. Instead, simple grows in its depth and meaning for me.

As a summary of the Christian faith, Luther's seal is simply Jesus, Christ crucified and risen, surrounded by faith and eternal life. The whole of the divine economy of salvation, the entirety of Holy Scripture, and the collection of all catechetical knowledge is summarized here. The Creator God is gracious toward self-condemned creatures. He has saved them through His Son (2 Corinthians 5:18–21), and He still seeks them by His Spirit (John 12:32; 15:26). He has imprinted His people on Himself (Isaiah 49:16), and He desires to imprint Himself on His people (Galatians 4:19; Ephesians 1:13).

Printing Luther's seal on things can be significant. It can provide a framework for reading Scripture, a picture of the Church's confession and identity, and the encouragement to remain focused on Christ at the center (Hebrews 12:1–2). Sealed things, however, are less significant than the imprint of this seal on you. On forehead and heart, God has sealed you with His grace and favor in Christ. He has sealed you with salvation and eternal life (Ephesians 4:30). Marked and sealed, you are called simply to live by faith (Galatians 2:20). It really is that simple.

CLOSING PRAYER: Dear Lord, You have sealed me with Your approval. May Your work for my salvation through Your Son, Jesus Christ, be imprinted on my body and soul that I might imprint every thought, word, and deed with the love of Jesus and the life He has given to me. In Jesus' name I pray. Amen.

The Church Year

God's people use the Church Year calendar to help them in their worship life. (Explanation, "The Church Year")

⊰∘⟨∽⟩∘⊱

One person esteems one day as better than another, while another esteems all days alike. Each one should be fully convinced in his own mind. (Romans 14:5)

LUTHER'S WRITINGS ON THE CHURCH YEAR

For the Epistles and Gospels we have retained the customary division according to the church year, because we do not find anything especially reprehensible in this use. And the present situation in Wittenberg is such that many are here who must learn to preach in places where this division is still being observed and may continue in force. Since in this matter we can be of service to others without loss to ourselves, we leave it, but have no objection to others who take up the complete books of the evangelists. This we think provides sufficient preaching and teaching for the lay people. He who desires more will find enough on other days.

AE 53:68

The Celebration of Each Day — Heidi Goehmann

Each of us has a favorite holiday, a favorite season, and favorite ways to observe and mark time. Christmas and Easter, beginnings and endings of years, the fervor of Pentecost, and the contemplation of Lent all have their place within our hearts and lives as we honor and celebrate all that God has done and all that God is doing. It can be easy to become stoic in our marking the days or attached to these markings in such a way that we miss their essence, their message, which is intended to gladden our hearts with each passing. We also can become so wrapped up in the busyness of life or the expectations of the celebration that we miss the heart of it.

Romans 14:5 reminds us that we all have preferences, and we can embrace our preferences, create our traditions, celebrate with our church families, and observe God's great goodness in our lives in our own ways. Luther goes on to remind us that knowing Jesus came, died for us, and rose again is sufficient without all the pomp and circumstance of any season, holiday, or celebration. He is the gift of every day. We rest in the words of Scripture to find our hope firmly in Christ not only during festivities, but also on Monday, Tuesday, Wednesday, Thursday, Friday, Saturday, and Sunday. We meet together in our homes, around our tables, and in our communities, marking each day as a celebration of His grace poured into our lives all 365 days of each and every year.

CLOSING PRAYER: Lord, You have created time and the seasons. You have given us the gift of celebrations and the joy of marking and remembering. Help us to acknowledge and praise what You have done in and outside of every day and season. You are our hope and our crown. In Jesus. Amen.

What Is Worship?

Why is it vital for us to gather together with fellow Christians in public worship?
The Word of God gathers all who believe in Jesus Christ into the Holy Christian Church, and also calls believers to gather together in congregations for public worship for several reasons. (Small Catechism, Question 52)

———— ⊶∘◠◡◠∘⊷ ————

But the hour is coming, and is now here, when the true worshipers will worship the Father in spirit and truth, for the Father is seeking such people to worship Him. God is spirit, and those who worship Him must worship in spirit and truth. (John 4:23–24)

LUTHER'S WRITINGS ON WORSHIP

We see, then, that the best and greatest part of all sacraments and of the mass is the words and promise of God, without which the sacraments are dead and are nothing at all, like a body without a soul, a cask without wine, a purse without money, a type without a fulfillment, a letter without the spirit, a sheath without a knife, and the like. Wherefore it is true that when we use, hear, or see the mass without the words or testament, and pay attention only to the sacrament and sign, we are not observing the mass even halfway. For sacrament without testament is a keeping of the case without the jewel, a quite one-sided separation and division.

AE 35:91

Why Worship, and How? — David Loy

The Christian life begins when the Holy Spirit, through God's Word, moves us to trust that the Father has forgiven our sins for Jesus' sake. It is sustained when the Spirit uses God's Word to show us our sins, move us to repentance, and announce forgiveness. Where does this happen? Certainly in personal devotions, but especially through other Christians in worship. There, God speaks to us through the pastor when he forgives our sins in Absolution and proclaims the Good News in the sermon. There, God speaks to us when we confess the Good News together in the Creed and sing it together in hymns and songs (see Colossians 3:16). We respond by praising God, offering prayers, and returning to our everyday lives to love our neighbors in our vocations (see Hebrews 10:24–25). The Spirit sustains our faith through God's Word.

This explains both why we should attend worship and what worship should be like. God commands us to share His Word with one another so that we grow in faith toward Him and love toward our neighbors. We need to hear His Law so we confess our sins, and we need to hear His Gospel so we cling to His forgiveness. Music, songs, and liturgy should therefore proclaim God's Word to us. Songs without the Gospel do not strengthen faith, and neither do rituals done for their own sake. Where song and ritual proclaim God's Word, however, the Spirit serves us and preserves us in the one true faith.

———— ⊶∘⧯∘⊷ ————

CLOSING PRAYER: Holy and everlasting Father, whenever we gather for worship, convict us of sin, move us to repentance, and create faith in Your forgiveness by Your Word and Spirit. Show us Jesus Christ crucified and risen from the dead in music, song, and liturgy. In the blessed name of Jesus. Amen.

Prayer

Martin Luther lays out a simple method for praying the words of the Ten Commandments, the Lord's Prayer, the Creed, or any text from the Bible. To help you remember, you might think of it as "I.T.C.P."

I nstruction
T hanksgiving
C onfession
P rayer

(SC, "Simple Prayer")

―――――∽o⚬◯⚬o∾―――――

Rejoice always, pray without ceasing, give thanks in all circumstances; for this is the will of God in Christ Jesus for you. (1 Thessalonians 5:16–18)

Luther's Writings on Prayer

But if you were to ask what you ought to bring up and bewail in your prayers, you could easily learn from the Ten Commandments and the Lord's Prayer. Open your eyes and look into your own life and into the life of all Christendom, particularly that of the spiritual estate. You will find how low faith, hope, love, obedience, chastity, and all virtue are, while all manner of heinous vice reigns supreme. You will find what a lack there is of good preachers and prelates; how only knaves, children, fools, and women rule. If you do this you will see that there is need every hour, everywhere, and without ceasing to pray with tears of blood to avert the terrible wrath of God. In fact it is true that there has never been a greater need of praying than at present and increasingly so until the end of the world.

AE 44:68–69

Such a Time as This — Heather Culli

Luther's words, "There has never been a greater need of praying than at present," seem as relevant today as they did five hundred years ago. News of wars, disasters, strife, and division threaten to overwhelm and paralyze even the strongest believer. Turning to God in prayer at times such as this can be especially comforting, but also exceedingly difficult. Where does one even begin? The needs seem so vast and the evil so rampant that a prayer list could go on indefinitely.

We need only turn to the Scriptures for the answer. Paul, writing in 1 Thessalonians, proposes a three-step plan. First and foremost, he invites us to rejoice. This seems almost trite when we view current events from an earthly perspective. But if we turn our thoughts to God and His Word, we are able to see His hand at work in the midst of chaos and rejoice in His goodness and strength. Second, Paul encourages believers to pray without ceasing. Bring everything to God in prayer—the good, the bad, and the ugly. Recall King David's heartfelt words to God in every season of his life. They ranged from songs of praise to accusatory rants, but God never despised them. The final step is to give thanks. This step requires us to look beyond what we desire to what God has already done. Our faith is made secure when we acknowledge His goodness in the past with thankful hearts for His good works.

—◦◦◦◦—

CLOSING PRAYER: Dear heavenly Father, Your love for us knows no bounds. You have promised to hear our prayers and answer according to Your good and gracious will. Help us when we lose heart. Send Your Holy Spirit to intercede on our behalf when we don't have the words to speak. Open our eyes to Your goodness, even in times of distress, and make us truly thankful. Amen.

Luther's Morning Prayer

I thank You, my heavenly Father, through Jesus Christ, Your dear Son, that You have kept me this night from all harm and danger; and I pray that You would keep me this day also from sin and every evil, that all my doings and life may please You. For into Your hands I commend myself, my body and soul, and all things. Let Your holy angel be with me, that the evil foe may have no power over me. Amen.

———⊶∘⊷∘⊶———

But I will sing of Your strength; I will sing aloud of Your steadfast love in the morning. For You have been to me a fortress and a refuge in the day of my distress. (Psalm 59:16)

LUTHER'S WRITINGS ON LUTHER'S MORNING PRAYER

It is a good thing to let prayer be the first business of the morning and the last at night. Guard yourself carefully against those false, deluding ideas which tell you, "Wait a little while. I will pray in an hour; first I must attend to this or that." Such thoughts get you away from prayer into other affairs which so hold your attention and involve you that nothing comes of prayer for that day.

It may well be that you may have some tasks which are as good or better than prayer, especially in an emergency. . . . Yet we must be careful not to break the habit of true prayer and imagine other works to be necessary which, after all, are nothing of the kind. Thus at the end we become lax and lazy, cool and listless toward prayer. The devil who besets us is not lazy or careless, and our flesh is too ready and eager to sin and is disinclined to the spirit of prayer.

AE 43:193, 194

What Do You Want for Me Today, Lord? — Scott Rauch

Praying is our faithful action believing that God is listening. We pray because we know that God is present and willing to be heard. How do we find this out? From Jesus. He faithfully and daily spends time with His Father, seeking His will for the day. Jesus tells us that He only does what the Father is doing. His Father wants only that ongoing relationship with us that acknowledges that He knows exactly what we need to be with Him and His creation. Jesus is content not to make things up for His daily life. He knows that whatever His Father thinks is best is good enough for Him.

Making use of a prayer like Luther's Morning Prayer, we have the opportunity to acknowledge God's presence in the past, day and night. Because of that faithful experience with Him, we boldly ask Him to lead us through the day to come. We humbly, and yet with childlike expectation, look forward to what He has in store for us. We ask for His protection from the evil one, who would see us distracted from the Lord and His blessings for us.

We can do all of this kind of praying because God is really present with us. Through the Holy Spirit's power, we speak with God in complete confidence that He loves us so much that nothing—not even our sin, the devil's power, and death—can defeat what He has in store for the day. Bring it on, Lord!

⚯

CLOSING PRAYER: Father in heaven, to You be all praise and glory. Rule in my life. Lead me well. Bring me what I need for today, especially the forgiveness bought by Jesus. Defend me against the evil one. I rejoice in You! In Jesus' name. Amen.

Luther's Evening Prayer

I thank You, my heavenly Father, through Jesus Christ, Your dear Son, that You have graciously kept me this day; and I pray that You would forgive me my sins where I have done wrong, and graciously keep me this night. For into Your hands I commend myself, my body and soul, and all things. Let Your holy angel be with me, that the evil foe may have no power over me. Amen.

———————— ◦◦◦◦ ————————

Let my prayer be counted as incense before You, and the lifting up of my hands as the evening sacrifice! (Psalm 141:2)

LUTHER'S WRITINGS ON LUTHER'S EVENING PRAYER

I still find it necessary every day to look for time during which I may pray. And I am satisfied if, when I retire, I can recite the Ten Commandments, pray the Lord's Prayer, and then add a Bible verse or two. Meditating on these, I fall asleep.

WLS § 3458

He Fills Us with Good Things — Faith Spelbring

A husband and wife were awoken in the middle of the night by their little boy. Half-awake and almost hysterical, he threw his arms around his parents and refused to let go. He had experienced a nightmare. As he told his parents what he had dreamed, they quickly realized that bits and pieces of his bad dream were from a movie they had watched before bed. The vivid pictures he had seen right before going to sleep had stayed with him and continued as he slept.

The couple decided that screen time would no longer happen right before bed. The director of their Sunday School program encouraged them to use bedtime as a family devotion time in which they would share about their day, read Scripture, and pray together. There was no promise that this would prevent nightmares going forward, but what the couple discovered was that their children went to bed with their parents' voices in their head, not an actor's. Rather than ingesting sarcastic words from teenage characters, their children went to bed having had God's Word poured over them. Best of all, the last thought of their day was of their Savior, Jesus, through whom they have direct access to God.

While God's people benefit from praying to Him at all times of day, evening prayers bless the hearts and minds of God's children of all ages and provide for them comfort and peace as they close their eyes to sleep. There is no better comfort than that.

⚬⚬◦⚮◦⚬⚬

CLOSING PRAYER: Dear heavenly Father, You invite Your children to call on Your name in prayer and fill them with Your peace. Through Christ, we have access to You and You do not turn us away. You chase away what threatens us and give us peace. Thank You for hearing our prayers. In Your holy name we pray. Amen.

Contributors

―⊶◦ᘓᘔ◦⊷―

Rev. Jonathan Boehne currently serves as pastor of Trinity Lutheran Church, El Paso, Illinois.

Heather Culli currently serves as fourth-grade teacher at Grace Lutheran School, Menomonee Falls, Wisconsin.

Heidi Goehmann, deaconess, LCSW, LIMHP, lives in Norfolk, Nebraska.

Rev. Dr. James Lamb currently serves as Life Advocate at Lutheran Family Service of Iowa, Fort Dodge, Iowa.

Rev. Dr. David Loy currently serves as associate dean of Christ College and associate professor of philosophy, theology, and ethics at Concordia University Irvine in California.

Scott Rauch, director of Christian education, currently serves at Trinity Lutheran Church, Peoria, Illinois.

Rev. Philip J. Rigdon currently serves as senior pastor of First Lutheran Church, Clearwater, Florida.

Rev. Jonathan Rusnak currently serves as pastor of Pilgrim Evangelical Lutheran Church, Wauwatosa, Wisconsin.

Faith Spelbring, director of Christian education, currently serves as executive director of the Association of Lutheran Mission Agencies (ALMA), Belleville, Illinois.

―⊶◦ᘓᘔ◦⊷―